With Jesus, the places of our deepest hur[t]
pected hope. Jodi Rosser has lived this firstl[y]
you can experience the same. With the voice of a friend and the wisdom of
experience, she'll come alongside you wherever you are today and help you
move toward healing one step at a time.

Holley Gerth
Bestselling Author of *What Your Heart Needs for the Hard Days*

When it comes to heartbreak, Jodi Rosser is an unintentional expert.
Having experienced the grief of a miscarriage, divorce, and the loss of
her friend to cancer, Jodi helps you see that your greatest heartbreak can
catapult you to your greatest growth. If you feel lost, broken, or far from
God, I highly recommend this book. Jodi's gentle voice, application of
Scripture, poignant questions, and sweet prayers will help you navigate
your own path of tragedy to find the Father's love. Grab your coffee and
settle into *Depth*—you won't regret a moment of it.

Jennifer Dukes Lee
Bestselling Author of *Growing Slow* and *It's All Under Control*

Depth is the book we all need when life hits with unexpected pain. Draw-
ing from her own deep experiences with loss, Jodi is the compassionate friend who sits with us in brokenness and vulnerability while gently
pointing us to hope. Each chapter is a tender step backed by scriptural
truth to make your way through losses you never saw coming. If you've
ever wondered how in the world you're going to make it through your
excruciating loss, *Depth* gives you steady encouragement with the needed
nudges not to waste this place of unwanted pain.

Lisa Appelo
Author of *Life Can Be Good Again: Putting Your World
Back Together After It All Falls Apart*

If you've experienced deep disappointment, a sudden crisis, unexpected grief, or unwanted pain, read *Depth: Growing Through Heartbreak to
Strength*. This book is filled with poignant true stories, powerful biblical
principles, practical action steps, and all the encouragement you need to
overcome obstacles and recapture hope. Jodi Rosser's vulnerability shines
through every page. Buy one copy for yourself and ten more to give away.

Carol Kent
Speaker and Author of *When I Lay My Isaac Down*

When suffering and hurt come into our lives, it's easy to wonder what's the purpose in the unexplained pain. Jodi Rosser compassionately invites us all to lean into God as He transforms our deepest heartaches into our greatest strengths. Written from a framework of biblical truths and understanding, this book is a must read for anyone wanting hope in the midst of hardship. God is the good and gracious Author of our stories. And He's not done yet.

Becky Beresford
Author, Speaker, Coach and Host of the *Brave Women Series*

Jodi Rosser has written a book that I wish I had when I grieved the loss of my daughter many years ago. If you are walking through heartbreak, grief, or disappointment, then this is the book for you. Jodi tenderly encourages each hurting heart with godly truth and points them back to our loving Father.

Sandra Maddox
Speaker, Children's Author, Contributor for *Chicken Soup for the Soul: Grieving and Recovery*

Tears filled my eyes as I read *Depth*—tears of both pain and joy. Have you ever felt deep heartbreak? Then you are in good company with Jodi Rosser. With honesty and vulnerability, she shares her sorrow through miscarriage, divorce, and loss of a loved one so that you can find hope in God again. I hope to share *Depth* with many women and plan to keep this book close at hand.

Noelle Hackney
Depth Launch Team Early Reader

Grief does not discriminate, and its reach knows no boundaries. *Depth: Growing through Heartbreak to Strength* is a resource for everyone. Each chapter begins with scripture and ends with prayer and a grief truth. Grief is a journey no one should walk alone. Jodi is the friend who grabs your hand and walks the road with you.

Wendy Pope
Speaker, Author, Founder and Executive Director of
Word Up Ministries

DEPTH

Joy,
  Praying this book helps
you grow deeper in your
faith! Thank you for all
your support & encouragement!
          D, Jodi
            Re

DEPTH

Growing Through

Heartbreak to Strength

JODI ROSSER

Dedication

*To the woman whose life
has just been shattered,*

*to the hurting heart
whose whole world changed
in an instant,*

*to the grieving soul
who struggles to get out of bed,*

*I understand. I see you.
I am one of you.
I wrote this book for you.*

Contents

Seek God and invite Him into the pain.

Tearfully allow yourself time to grieve and process the emotions.

Replace your finite view with God's infinite perspective.

Embrace God's character development in the midst of the chaos.

Never lose sight of God's grace.

Give praise to God even as your heart breaks.

Trust God is good when your mind is doubting and you don't understand.

Honestly share your story and help another hurting heart.

Foreword

By Kathe Wunnenberg

"God, use my hurt to bring hope to help others!"

This was my heart's cry many years ago in the midst of gut-wrenching grief. After years of infertility, a miscarriage, and adopting a child, I discovered I was pregnant. My joy quickly turned to sorrow when I learned my baby had a fatal birth defect. For twenty-eight more weeks, I carried my unborn child, knowing God could heal him, yet trusting Him with the outcome that would glorify Him the most. After a long, intense labor, John Samuel was born. Within a few hours heaven's gates opened and welcomed him into the arms of Jesus. His brief life has touched multitudes around the world, and the ripple effects will only be known in eternity.

Little did I know when I cried out to God to use my hurt to bring hope to others, that He would open the doors for me to write, speak, and start a Hopelifters ministry. Amazingly, Jodi Rosser read my devotional book, *Grieving the Child I Never Knew,* after the loss of her baby. Although Jodi and I didn't officially meet until years later when she invited me to be on her podcast in 2020, God connected our hearts long ago through heartbreak. This made

it easy for our friendship to ignite into an intentional, growing, purpose-driven connection, which it is today. We also share a passion to encourage brokenhearted women who need hope and have a story to share that can help others.
Perhaps that is you.

The book you hold in your hand, *Depth: Growing through Heartbreak to Strength,* is living proof of God's faithfulness to use your pain for purpose, transform your hurt into hope, and grow you through your heartbreak to strength. Like a friend sitting across from you having coffee, Jodi Rosser's authentic sharing, personal stories, practical insights, prayers, and truth to replace lies will encourage and inspire you. Her friendship with Jesus and her deep faith is evident and contagious.

I believe we go through what we go through so we can help others go through what we went through.

God used my heartbreak to strengthen me and also Jodi. God used Jodi's heartbreak to strengthen her, and it will also strengthen you.

I am praying 2 Corinthians 1:3–4 for you. "May the Father of compassion and the God of all comfort, who comforts us in all our troubles, so that we can comfort those in any trouble with the comfort we ourselves have received from God." May God touch multitudes through this book.

Turn the page and begin your healing journey.

1

When Your Heart Shatters

He heals the brokenhearted
and binds up their wounds.
Psalm 147:3

I still remember every detail like it was just yesterday.
Alone in my car, I started fidgeting with the volume button on the CD player. Not even the worship song could take away how I felt as I drove to my doctor's office for my sixteen-week appointment. Another red light, another delay on the road to finding answers. It seemed like an eternity for the light to turn green. These last couple of weeks had felt the same. My mind started racing once again. *What if something is wrong? What if my gut feeling is correct?*

I hit the gas pedal as the light turned green. I needed to get to my doctor's office as quickly as possible. When I was there four weeks earlier, my doctor confirmed that everything was fine with my baby. But now, I could not get past this persistent feeling that there was a problem. Even though I did not have any negative symptoms, I just sensed it in my core.

Tapping my finger on the steering wheel at every stoplight and stop sign, I counted down the minutes. I thought back to the first time I was pregnant. From high blood pressure during my first trimester to complications that led to bed rest the third trimester, my pregnancy with my oldest son, Kyle, was anything but uneventful. Thankfully, this pregnancy had been different. My blood pressure was normal; the heartbeat was strong. Both the doctor and I were thrilled there were no complications at twelve weeks.

I remember smiling as I pictured Kyle's sweet face when we told him the exciting news weeks earlier. He could not wait to have a baby brother or sister. He wore his new "I am going to be a big brother" T-shirt proudly as I snapped a picture of him in our family room. I attached the picture, along with the twelve-week ultrasound baby picture, to an email sharing our thrilling news with everyone we knew. Our family was growing!

I wish I felt that same excitement now.

As I pulled into the parking lot, I could not get my mind to slow down. *If something were terribly wrong, my body would have shown me. I would be cramping or bleeding. Since I have no signs of trouble, then I must be fine. Then my baby must be fine too.* Oh, how I wished this logic would calm my anxious heart. As I put my car in park, I hoped I was about to get some answers.

Lying alone on the bed in the exam room, I could not wait for the doctor to arrive. The room was quiet and sterile. Honestly, it was too silent; I just wanted to hear the sound of my baby's heartbeat. The ten-minute wait seemed like hours.

As the door opened, the doctor asked me how I was feeling. I told her my concerns, so she immediately placed the Doppler, a baby heartbeat monitor, near the top of my belly. We both listened intently as she moved it up and down my stomach. There was no sound from the baby. Moving it to the left and to the right, there was still no heartbeat. Sadly, the only sound in the room was the Doppler picking up my own heartbeat, which was speeding up each second.

Panic began to rise inside me as all my worries and fears were becoming a reality.

After five long minutes, the doctor stopped and calmly told me she wanted to look at the baby on an ultrasound. I was anything but calm. My heart was pounding, and my mind was spinning out of control. *Oh no! What if my baby stopped growing?* Scared, I realized I probably should not have come to this appointment alone. Tears filled my eyes as I tried to make sense of what was happening.

The doctor led me to the ultrasound room next door. As the technician immediately showed the sonogram, my eyes focused on my precious baby. Knowing where to look for the heartbeat, I stared closely at the monitor. My heart shattered when I did not see a heartbeat flickering on the screen. My whole world changed in an instant.

I was devastated.

My hopes and dreams for this new life were over before they even began.

Tears started streaming down my face.

My heart was breaking.

Have you ever felt heartbreak? Deep heartbreak?

Maybe you have lost a loved one to cancer or suicide, and you miss her every day as you are filled with deep grief.

Perhaps your marriage is ending in a divorce, and you feel intense hurt from the one person you thought would love you the rest of your life.

It could be that you longed to be married, but years go by, and you are still single and feeling alone.

Maybe your heart desires to be a mom, but each month, the same negative answer comes up on the pregnancy test, and you feel disappointed.

Perhaps you've lost a friendship, a job, or a dream for you or your child, and you are feeling discouraged.

Heartbreak comes when life does not end up the way you planned or expected. These disappointments are very real and can leave you feeling like there is a deep hole in your soul. What do you do when life takes these unexpected turns and leaves you heartbroken? How do you walk through these storms and come out on the other side stronger than when you entered the storm? How do you handle loss, grief, and disappointment in your life?

I know it is not easy. Grief is the hardest emotion to navigate. For me, it felt like my heart was being shattered into a million pieces, and I didn't know where to start or how to pick up the pieces to move forward. If you are feeling the same way, then I am so thankful you picked up this book. I want to help you heal from your heartbreak in a healthy way. But I also want you to grow deep roots as God redeems your pain. I believe depth in your faith is one the greatest gifts in the middle of the heartbreak.

I don't know where you are right now on your journey. You could be in the middle of a storm grieving a loss, just coming out of a storm healing from a loss, or facing a storm on the horizon. Wherever you are, I want to come alongside you and let you know that you are not alone. Storms have a way of making you feel lonely, as if no one else has gone through what you have experienced. This is not true.

If you are in the middle of the storm grieving a loss, I am so sorry you are going through this. I know firsthand how hard it is, and my heart is deeply saddened for you. I wish I could reach through the pages of this book and give you a big hug. I know the heartbreak is real, and it deeply hurts.

I am truly sorry that your mom passed away even though your hope was for her to be healed.

I am truly sorry that your marriage ended even though your hope was to grow old with your spouse.

I am truly sorry that you are still single even though your hope is to be married.

I am truly sorry that you are struggling to get pregnant or perhaps have miscarried even though your hope was to have a healthy baby.

WHEN YOUR HEART SHATTERS

I am truly sorry that you lost your job even though your hope was to provide for your family.

Friend, I understand the deep pain you are feeling because I have experienced three great heartbreaks in my life:

- I suffered a miscarriage of my sweet baby girl.
- I endured a heartbreaking divorce that shattered my dreams for my family.
- I held my best friend's hand as pancreatic cancer took her young life.

Each heartbreak challenged me beyond what I thought I could handle. Just like you, I have cried buckets of tears over these losses. Just like you, I have found it difficult to find hope in the middle of the hurt. Just like you, I have cried out to God, wondering how He can bring good out of these difficult circumstances. I have asked the hard questions too. *Why is this happening to me? Where is God in these storms? How will I get through this?*

Throughout these pages, I will share my stories with you, but more importantly, I will give you some inspiring truths God has shown me along my path from heartbreak to strength. I know the road is not easy. It involves intentionality on your part and surrendering to God. It means trusting God through times of refinement and growth even when it does not all make sense. There will be tears, frustrations, and times you want to give up along the way. But there will also be moments when you are awestruck by the God of the universe. I cannot wait for you to see how much He loves you and cares about even the smallest details of your life.

I have created a powerful acrostic for the word *strength*. Each letter presents an important action step that will help you process your loss in a healthy way. We will dive deeper into each of these in the chapters to follow.

Seek God and invite Him into your pain.

Tearfully allow yourself time to grieve and process the emotions.

Replace your finite view with God's infinite perspective.

Embrace God's character development in the midst of the chaos.

Never lose sight of God's grace.

Give praise to God even as your heart breaks.

Trust God is good when your mind is doubting and you don't understand.

Honestly share your story and help another hurting heart.

Please understand that these eight action steps take years to live out; they are not quick items on a checklist. Walking through heartbreak is hard, and healing takes time and intentionality. Grief is never linear; there will be times when you are making good progress, and then a memory or trigger will cause a setback. Remember that healing is a journey, and the goal is progress. These steps helped me along my journey, and my desire is they will do the same for you.

Remember that healing is a journey, and the goal is progress.

My prayer is that these action steps will lead you directly into the arms of Jesus, because only He can heal your broken heart and restore your soul. I also pray that the truth statements and prayers at the end of each chapter will offer you comfort and peace as you grieve and heal from your pain. I want to ignite within you a desire to grow into the person God has created you to be so you can live out your purpose. As you cultivate these deep roots, I pray God can use your hurts and pain to help someone else going through the same storm.

Friend, as I wrote this book for you, there were lots of tears shed. Some came from remembering the hurt and grief, but most were tears of hope. Hope that God can turn your pain into His purpose. Hope that God has a good plan to grow you even when you cannot see how good can come from this. Hope that your broken story will help another hurting heart.

Looking back at my grief, books were a huge part of my healing, so I pray this book is part of your healing too! I have discovered that God never wastes a hurt. As you fully surrender and depend on God in the middle of your heartbreaking circumstance, I know God can take you from a place of heartbreak to strength. Let me leave you with this question to think about as you read through these pages: "What if your greatest heartbreak catapults you to your greatest growth?"

Each chapter ends with a prayer, and I would love to pray these words over you right now.

Let's Pray

> *God*, I want to lift up the hurting soul who is reading this book. I know in the midst of the devastation, it is hard to see how You can redeem all of the tears and pain. Please wrap Your loving arms around her grieving heart and remind her she is not alone. Empower her daily as she begins this healing journey. Allow her time to process the hurt as she seeks You and help her develop depth in her faith. Take this heartbreak and turn it into the strength that only You can give. In Jesus's name, Amen.

Truth

> Healing takes time and intentionality.

<u>S</u>eek God and invite Him into your pain.

<u>T</u>earfully allow yourself time to grieve and process the emotions.

<u>R</u>eplace your finite view with God's infinite perspective.

<u>E</u>mbrace God's character development in the midst of the chaos.

<u>N</u>ever lose sight of God's grace.

<u>G</u>ive praise to God even as your heart breaks.

<u>T</u>rust God is good when your mind is doubting and you don't understand.

<u>H</u>onestly share your story and help another hurting heart.

2

Closer Than You Think

The Lord is close to the brokenhearted
and saves those who are crushed in spirit.
Psalm 34:18

It was the worst day of my life.

Lying alone in my king-sized bed, I tossed and turned. The clock mocked me as the hours read one, then two, then three in the morning. Now it was 4:00 a.m., and I hadn't slept a wink. My mind kept replaying the events of the evening over and over in my head. I still could not believe that this was the end.

Just hours earlier, I had stood there shocked by what my husband told me. I did not want to believe what I was hearing. Honestly, I had not been this devastated since my miscarriage eight years before.

Like a ton of bricks crashing over my body, the weight of his words seemed unbearable. Each utterance hurt as if a sword pierced my heart. I wanted to escape, but I felt completely paralyzed.

As though coming face-to-face with a mountain lion, my instincts kicked in. My choice was fight or flight. With adrenaline pumping through my body, I had to get away from this giant predatory-sized pain chasing after me. I bolted for the stairs thinking, *I don't want to be divorced.*

In the safety of my bedroom, I called my accountability partner, Erin, to share the heartbreaking news. Tears streaming down my face, I knew I would not be able to handle this alone. I needed her help.

As the phone was ringing, I thought back to the weekly walks Erin and I had been taking together the past several months to purposefully pray for healing in my marriage. I was truly hopeful that God could restore us, but now it looked bleak. When she answered the phone, I sobbed as I shared that my marriage of fifteen years was over.

I will never forget that night.

It was the night when my heart was shattered.

It was the night when my hopes and dreams for my family seemed to die.

It was the night when life turned upside down.

I could not see how I was going to get through this. Not only was my life going to completely change, but my kids' lives would be forever changed too. All I could think about was my two children. *Just the thought of them growing up in a divorced home crushes me.*

"Dear God," I prayed, "please watch over my kids during this uncertain time and protect them. Guard their hearts and minds, allow them to grieve the loss in a healthy way, and let them know how much I love them." After writing those words in my journal, I cried out again to the Lord, "How are we going to get through this? I don't even know what to do."

Have you ever felt alone and afraid as you faced an impossible circumstance? Maybe your life is whirling out of control, and you are grasping for answers. Perhaps it is difficult to see any light in the middle of your darkness.

I understand. That night, I began enduring the hardest year of my life.

The morning after my life took an unexpected turn, I went digging through my desk. I remembered hearing a series at my church just months earlier called "Getting Through What You're Going Through." Pastor Rick Warren had just come back from a hiatus as he grieved the loss of his youngest son. He had just suffered through the greatest heartbreak of his life, and his sermons were some of the most profound and amazing messages he has ever shared. Little did I know then how much I was going to need his wisdom.

Searching for the sermon notes, I read the words I had written on the top of the outline: "God uses pain to fulfill the purposes of your life." Not at all sure how He was going to do that, I kept reading. One of his bullet points said, "I can use my pain to draw closer to God." In the margin, I had scribbled, "You have a choice: you can run to God or run away from God."

There is something about being taken to a place of heartbreak where you have to choose either to run to God with your pain or run away from God in anger. At that moment, I chose to run to the Lord with my pain: every hour, every day, or every minute if necessary.

I put down the sermon notes, grabbed my pen, and wrote this in my journal:

> *God*, I truly want to grow from my pain. I don't want it to break me. I want it to grow me and help me draw closer to you. Only you can give me strength in this nightmare I am living. Only you can turn my tears into hope. I lay this at your feet. Please take my pain and help me draw closer to you, your power, your strength, your love, and your comfort. Help me to teach my kids to do that too. Help me be an example to them and give me the strength for another day.

I am not going to tell you that life suddenly got easier. I was facing a real storm. The waves kept crashing and the winds kept blowing. I can tell you this: God is faithful. He did give me strength each day, and He can do the same for you. As I cried out to Him each morning, He met me right where I was. Heartbroken. Hurting. Devastated.

He gave me comfort when I felt alone.

He gave me strength to help comfort my kids.

He gave me power to help me get through each day.

Looking back now, I don't know how I got through those first weeks and months. Honestly, I just started with one simple step: inviting God into my pain each day. Sometimes I breathed a quick prayer. "Help me, God, today, I don't have the strength." Other days, I got up before my kids and journaled. Most often, I clung to a verse that reminded me I was not alone in my grief.

I needed these reminders constantly. Like water to my thirsty soul, I wanted to know that I was not facing this pain alone. On my hard days, it became vital to remember that God was walking step by step with me. Focusing on God's presence, not my problems, was a theme in many of the devotionals I was reading. They pointed me to Scripture verses that filled my mind with truth.

The God of the universe was inviting me each day to walk through my problems with Him. He is inviting you too.

Will you surrender your heartbreak to Him?

Will you turn to God and run to Him in the middle of your pain?

Will you seek Him daily to give you strength and let your roots grow deeper in Him?

Listen to Him calling to you:

> "Be strong and courageous. Do not be afraid or terrified because of them, for the Lord your God goes with you; he will never leave you nor forsake you." (Deuteronomy 31:6)
>
> *Speak this truth:* "God wants me to know that I am not facing this alone."

> "My Peace I give you . . . Do not let your heart be troubled." (John 14:27)
>
> *Speak this truth:* "God wants to give me His peace in exchange for my troubled heart."

"Fear not, for I have redeemed you; I have called you by name, you are mine. When you pass through the waters, I will be with you; and through the rivers, they shall not overwhelm you; when you walk through fire you shall not be burned, and the flame shall not consume you. For I am the Lord your God, the Holy One of Israel, your Savior." (Isaiah 43:1–3 ESV)

Speak this truth: "God wants to walk alongside me through my storm."

"God is our refuge and strength, an ever-present help in trouble. Therefore we will not fear, though the earth give way and the mountains fall into the heart of the sea, though its waters roar and foam and the mountains quake with their surging." (Psalm 46:1–3)

Speak this truth: "God wants to strengthen me and help me in my times of trouble."

"But I will call on God, and the Lord will rescue me. Morning, noon, and night I cry out in my distress, and the Lord hears my voice." (Psalm 55:16-17 NLT)

Speak this truth: "God wants me to know He hears me as I cry out to Him."

(Note: I have created a special resource, "10 Verses to Help Encourage Your Hurting Heart." See Appendix A.)

I recommend writing these Scriptures on notecards and putting them on your bathroom mirror or hanging them on the refrigerator. As I placed these verses around my computer screen, I saw them daily as I wrote and checked my email. Some of my friends have verses on the dashboard of their car to help them declare God's truth during their daily commute. I encourage you to pick the one that most speaks to you. Honestly, you need God's truth in your mind and heart every day as you navigate through your storm.

The time I spent daily with God directly influenced my ability to handle my heartbreaking emotions during my grief.

Most mornings, I woke up tired and fatigued with the weight of the world on my shoulders. I did not have enough physical and emotional strength to weather the storm I was facing. I needed to rely on God's strength. I wish I could say that I carved out time every morning. But many days, life just took off, and I did not spend one minute filling up with God's truth before the busy began.

I remember sharing with my friend at my weekly small group about one particular day when this happened. Wednesday mornings at church were such a breath of fresh air in my week, and Bible study had just ended. Sitting outside on a bench near the tent where we just sang and worshipped, I confided in her how hard my yesterday had been. My emotions were heightened, and the sadness was more intense than days before. Loneliness had penetrated my soul, and I felt like Eeyore with a cloud of despair over my head. I think I had started to fall into self-pity.

The more we talked, the more I realized that I had tried to weather those strong feelings in my own strength that day, and I fell short. That night, as I collapsed in bed exhausted, I wrote in my journal, "God, forgive me for trying to do it all myself. I cannot get through this on my own. Lord, I need you every day." I was learning total dependence on God.

When the difficulties of life are closing in around you, run to God to break free. He wants to help you in your greatest time of need. I love Psalm 34:18. It tells me "The Lord is close to the brokenhearted and saves those who are crushed in spirit." God is near to us in our heartbreak.

Closeness shows God's desire for intimacy.
Closeness shows God's loving character.
Closeness shows God's helping hand.

The Lord wants to meet you in your pain in a way you never knew possible. I found this prayer in my journal, and I think it is a great place to start. In the middle

The Lord wants to meet you in your pain in a way you never knew possible.

of your tears, cry out to Him and say, "God, I am running to you with my arms wide open. I need you to get me through this tough time. Please help me keep my mind and my thoughts focused on you and you alone."

Friend, I believe walking through heartbreak on your own is nearly impossible. But walking through heartbreak with God alongside you and even carrying you leads you to place of great strength. So, keep running to God daily and surrendering your heartbreak to Him. Focus on God's presence, not your problems. Remember He is close to the brokenhearted, and He will strengthen you during the storm.

Let's Pray

God, I don't want to walk through this heartbreak alone. Thank You for holding me close as my world has been turned upside down. I need You more than ever. I don't know how to move forward, so I am asking You to meet me in my pain and deepen my faith in You. Give me Your power and energy today as I seek you. Fill me with Your love and comfort and help me focus on Your presence in the middle of this storm. God, I know I cannot do this in my own strength, so I need Your strength to make it through today. In Jesus's name, Amen.

Truth

Your time spent daily with God directly influences your ability to handle your heartbreaking emotions.

3

One Word Can Change Everything

Do not be anxious about anything,
but in every situation, by prayer and petition,
with thanksgiving, present your requests to God.
And the peace of God, which transcends
all understanding, will guard your hearts
and your minds in Christ Jesus.

Philippians 4:6–7

I hung up the phone in disbelief.

My stomach was in knots over what I had just heard. My mind kept repeating over and over, *This cannot be happening,* and each time, the words kept getting louder and louder. I plopped down on my couch, completely disheartened. It was like all the air was deflating out of me. All I could think about was my sweet friend, Jeannie. We had been through so much together.

She had walked faithfully with me from the beginning of my divorce just two years before. Now, tears flooded my eyes as I remembered the first time we met at MOPS (Mothers of Preschoolers) when our older kids were both two years old. We immediately connected, especially as she emotionally opened up to me about

her difficult summer. Sadly, Jeannie had lost her baby girl, Ga-
briella, six months into the pregnancy. We wept together over the
heartbreaking details of her loss and grief.

I did not know what to say since at that time I had not yet
walked through my own miscarriage. I wished I knew another
woman who had experienced something similar so she could offer
comfort to Jeannie. Then, just weeks later, our MOPS table leader
shared her testimony revealing she had also lost a baby. I remember
sitting there in awe of how God had orchestrated placing Jeannie at
that exact table at that exact time, knowing our table leader would
be able to relate directly to her pain.

Little did I know then that God had placed me at that table for
the same reason. When I lost my baby the following summer, Jeannie was the first person I called after my family. I knew she would
be able to completely understand and bring me comfort and hope.
Jeannie was a faith friend, one who continued to point me back to
my faith in the Lord during both good and difficult times.

As fall arrived, Jeannie and I were both thrilled to be expecting
at the same time. Her son was due in December, and my son was
due in May. Excited that our boys would be the same age, since our
oldest children were already two months apart, I looked forward to
doing life together with my good friend.

As I sat on my couch, the words from her phone call changed
everything. For the past month, Jeannie had been experiencing a
lot of pain. Frustrated that the doctors could not figure out what
was going on, I had called her each day to see if she had been given
any answers. Neither of us was expecting to find out that she had
pancreatic cancer.

As this shocking diagnosis crushed my heart, I committed to be
there for my friend through the fierce storm she was about to face.

There are some words that change your life forever. *Cancer* is one of those words.

Have you ever received a phone call that left you shocked and scared?

Has the dreadful word *cancer* interrupted your life or that of a loved one?

Have life's circumstances left you wondering what your future holds?

Not knowing what would happen next for Jeannie, my mind flooded with what-ifs. What if her cancer has already spread too much in her body? What if her kids grow up without their mom? What if I lose my dear friend? Maybe you have asked your own set of what-if questions.

Worry began to take root with each negative thought. My emotions spiraled out of control as anxiety for my friend turned into feeling stressed about her kids. Very quickly, I was overcome with fear.

What do you do when the hard circumstances of life give birth to what-ifs? How do you not get stuck in those anxious places when you face something severe like a cancer diagnosis? How do you break free when fear has a firm hold on you?

In Philippians 4:6, the Bible says, "Do not be anxious about anything." I have read that entire verse many times. In fact, this is the life verse for my youngest son, Conor. But in the light of Jeannie's cancer diagnosis, this passage became extremely hard to live out. My mind was whirling with anxious thoughts. Maybe your mind is too.

Max Lucado shed some great insight on Philippians 4 in his book *Anxious for Nothing*. He pointed out that the verse is referring to perpetual anxiety, and God does not want us in a constant place of fear. He says, "The presence of anxiety is unavoidable, but the prison of anxiety is optional."[1]

Thankfully, it is not God's desire for us to live in bondage to our worries.

I also think it is helpful to look at Philippians 4:5. Right before the well-known passage to not be anxious, it reads, "The Lord is near." Verses 5 and 6 have been separated, but Paul wrote these words to be read together, making them much more powerful. Listen to them as one continual thought: "The Lord is near, so do not be anxious about anything."

Because the Lord is near, you don't have to be worried. Since God is close to the brokenhearted, you don't have to stay stuck in anxiety. This is much easier said than done, so it requires you to be intentional and practical.

The next time you start to have an anxious thought, I encourage you to write it down in a journal. On one side of the page, list your negative thoughts. On the other side, gather a promise from Scripture that will help you focus on truth instead of fear. For example: Jeannie's cancer diagnosis left me feeling worried. I wrote, "I am worried" on the left side of the page. Then, I looked for a verse to reset my focus, and I chose 1 Peter 5:7(NLT). "Give all your worries and cares to God, for he cares about you."

Here is some of the common negative chatter we tell ourselves alongside a verse in the Bible we can use to fix our thoughts. When I lost my baby, I felt very alone, so I regularly reminded myself God would never leave me, nor forsake me (Hebrews 13:5). As a single parent, I often feel like I can't do it on my own, so I need to change my thinking by recalling that I can do all things through Christ who gives me strength (Philippians 4:13). Find the thoughts and verses that relate to you and write them down in your journal.

THOUGHTS	GOD'S TRUTH
I feel all alone	"I will never leave you nor forsake you." (Hebrews 13:5 ESV)
I can't do this.	"I can do all things through Christ who gives me strength." (Philippians 4:13 BSB)
I am worried.	"Give all your worries and cares to God, for he cares about you." (1 Peter 5:7 NLT)
I am tired.	"Come to me, all you who are weary and burdened, and I will give you rest." (Matthew 11:28)
I feel weak.	"He gives strength to the weary and increases the power of the weak." (Isaiah 40:29)
I don't have answers.	"If any of you lacks wisdom, you should ask God, who gives generously to all without finding fault, and it will be given to you." (James 1:5).
I am afraid.	"Have I not commanded you? Be strong and courageous. Do not be afraid; do not be discouraged, for the Lord your God will be with you wherever you go." (Joshua 1:9)
I want to give up.	"Let us not become weary in doing good, for at the proper time we will reap a harvest if we do not give up." (Galatians 6:9)

There is power in quoting God's Word over your life. I highly recommend you memorize the verse that speaks the most truth into your pain. Combating those anxious thoughts with Scripture will help tremendously. You may feel tired and weak in the middle of your storm. Perhaps you don't have the strength to keep going, and you are ready to give up. Try moving your eyes off your problem and onto God.

You can daily surrender your heartbreaking thoughts to God and allow Him to fill your mind with His truth. As you release each thought and trust Him, you are growing your roots deeper in Him.

Let's look at the entire set of verses in Philippians 4:5–8.

> Let your gentleness be evident to all. The Lord is near. Do not be anxious about anything, but in every situation, by prayer and petition, with thanksgiving, present your requests to God. And the peace of God, which transcends all understanding, will guard your hearts and your minds in Christ Jesus. Finally, brothers and sisters, whatever is true, whatever is noble, whatever is right, whatever is pure, whatever is lovely, whatever is admirable—if anything is excellent or praiseworthy—think about such things.

In that final verse, Philippians 4:8, some Bible translations say, "Fix your thoughts on what is true." I like this word *fix* because it shows that we have a choice in what we think about.

Max Lucado gave a great analogy to help us understand this better. He refers to our minds as a mental airport, and we are the traffic controller. As the control tower directs airport traffic, we also direct the mental traffic in our minds. Our thoughts will start circling above just like planes circle over an airport, and we can choose which ones we allow to land. We can also decide which ones we direct to take off and fly away.[2]

Friend, we are in control of our thought patterns. We determine what thoughts get to land and what thoughts we send off.

Just because the thought enters our mind does not mean we need to give it power to put down roots and occupy space.

> **We cannot control our circumstances, but we can control our thoughts.**

So, what are you fixing on? Will you fix your thoughts on what is true, noble, right, pure, lovely, admirable, excellent, and praiseworthy? Or will you fixate on what-if statements, worries, anxieties, and stresses in your life?

We cannot control our circumstances, but we can control our thoughts. We cannot change what is happening to us, but we can change how we are going to think about it.

I am not going to lie. Jeannie's cancer diagnosis rattled me, and I allowed negative thoughts to land in my mind. Maybe you have allowed worry to occupy space in your mind too.

Just like an air traffic controller, it is time to tell that plane to take off. It no longer has permission to land in your mental airport. I know this is not easy, and you will probably find yourself making progress for a couple of days and then backtracking: two steps forward, three steps back. The key is to not get stuck in the prison of anxiety. Keep using Scripture to combat each thought. Take every anxious thought captive, so it does not take you captive.

Let's Pray

> *God*, I am so thankful for the truth in the Bible that helps us combat each negative thought. I ask for Your strength to take control of the negative chatter that circles my mind and wants to land. Help me use Scripture to test each thought to see if it is true, noble, right, pure, lovely, admirable, excellent, and praiseworthy. I don't want to live in a state of worry and anxiety. God, I know there is power in Your Word. I ask You today to fill my mind with Your truth so that I may deepen my faith in You! In Jesus's name, Amen.

Truth

> Your circumstances are out of your control, but the way you think about them is in your control.

4

God Provides

*My God will meet all your needs according
to the riches of his glory in Christ Jesus.*
Philippians 4:19

I could not believe the words coming out of her mouth.

The walk from the ultrasound room back to my exam room was a blur. Passing other pregnant women in the hallway seemed like a cruel joke. Their smiles and carefree laughter deeply contrasted with my crying and confusion. I kept wondering, *Why had my baby stopped growing?* Like gazing through a window to the outside world, others could see my heartbreaking story as they looked upon my red, puffy eyes. I could not hold back my tears.

Alone in the exam room, I frantically searched in my purse for the phone to call my family to share the devastating news. I called my husband first, and he immediately jumped in his car to come join me. On the second call to my mom, I could barely get the words out of my mouth in between the sobbing. I managed to muster, "The baby is gone."

Crying could be heard on the other end of the phone, and I knew she completely understood the pain I was experiencing. Sadly, mom had walked a similar path, having had two miscarriages before my oldest sister was born. We wept for all the hopes and dreams we had for this baby—hopes and dreams that had vanished as quickly as her life began.

Exhausted, I collapsed on the hard bed, waiting for the doctor to arrive and tell me the next step. Would I need to have surgery? Would they need to induce me? Completely confused, I thought, *Why did my body hold on tightly to this baby if she was no longer alive and thriving?* In the midst of the whirlwind of questions and worry, I heard a knock on the door.

Just when I thought it could not get any worse, the doctor entered the room completely void of any emotion. I expected her to be warm and comforting, but instead the words that came out of her mouth were blunt, cold, and heartless. "I cannot help you anymore."

There was no compassion or understanding flowing from her lips. No, "I am so sorry for your loss." No empathy or tenderness in her delivery. They were just unsympathetic words followed by an abrupt recommendation that I go to a Family Planning Clinic to have my baby removed since I was in my second trimester.

Her horrifying solution to my dilemma brought more tears to my already bloodshot eyes. I was astonished by her lack of bedside manner. *Why is my doctor abandoning me in my greatest time of need?* This same woman who had walked with me every step of the way through the complications of Kyle's pregnancy had just left me helpless and alone.

My day of sorrow was quickly becoming a day of shock and distress.

Completely defeated, I dragged myself out of the doctor's office and met my husband in the parking lot. We called our parents, sisters, and small group to share the doctor's appalling plan. Stunned and shaken, none of us were comfortable with going to the Family Planning Clinic. *This baby inside of me was not unwanted. This baby was planned, and a gift to our family. The last place I want to step foot into is an abortion clinic.* It made me cry even harder.

Some friends had shared with us that lines of pro-lifers picket in front of the clinic. The thought of people thinking I was having an abortion when my real circumstances were completely opposite was devastating. With hope quickly draining from me, I prayed for God to show me another way.

Do you find yourself in a situation right now that feels out of your control? Are you wondering, "Where is God?" and "Why is this happening?"

There are times in your life when your circumstances are more than you can bear. Your heart is breaking, and you feel completely alone and abandoned. It is in these exact moments that you can turn toward God. You can invite him into your pain and pray for His wisdom, guidance, and truth to be revealed. You can ask Him for comfort, love, and grace as you walk the hard road set before you.

The good news is that you do not have to walk it alone. God is faithfully walking alongside you. He wants to help and provide for you when you are in need.

You just have one brave choice to make. You can either run toward God or run away from Him. From experience, I will tell you that the first choice will bring you peace in the middle of your storm. The second choice leaves you to weather the storm alone.

The brave choice is to invite the God of the universe to journey with you through your pain, focusing on His presence, not your problems. Bravery is leaning into God when your life's circumstances are falling apart around you.

That sorrowful day, I made the courageous choice. I invited God to help me as I asked my family and friends to pray for another option to be revealed.

The brave choice is to invite the God of the universe to journey with you through your pain.

Friend, God is faithful! He showed up in ways I never knew possible! He provided for me in my time of need, and I know He wants to do the same for you. Remember, you are not alone in your loss. God hears you and has not forgotten you.

After a long day of phone calls, I collapsed on the couch. Exhausted and exasperated from getting the run around from both my doctor's office and the insurance company, I was running out of options. I honestly was about to give up when my phone rang.

My mom's name popped up on the screen. *Please have some good news,* I thought as I answered. She told me about a doctor and his family from our old church. Their son was in the high school group back when my husband and I mentored students years earlier. They were appreciative to us for working with their son that after hearing our predicament, the father, Dr. Linzey, offered to meet us at his office for an ultrasound the next morning. He was not sure if he could help, but he was willing to try.

A glimmer of hope was peeking through the dark clouds of my storm. We were so grateful for his offer. Optimistically, I thought, *He could be the answer to our prayer!*

Ironically, I once again found myself in a car in route to the doctor's office. This time, I was not alone; my husband was driving. Surprisingly, I was not anxious like before either. Instead, I was overcome with an indescribable peace. God was providing for me in ways I could not understand.

The office was quiet and empty that early Saturday morning. As I saw the hundreds of cute baby pictures on the walls, I knew I was in good hands. Dr. Linzey switched on the ultrasound machine, and an image of our sweet baby appeared on the monitor. I studied the picture on the screen. It was so special to see our precious angel again. I was so focused on finding a heartbeat during the last ultrasound that I had not looked closely at the outline of her face. She was beautiful.

While I was captivated by her photo, the doctor was busy measuring the baby's size and analyzing all the data to see if he could help us. Most doctors are hesitant to perform surgery after the first trimester because there is a risk to the mother as the baby's bones start to harden. After his review, the doctor shared that the baby had passed away around week 13–14, even though I was sixteen weeks along in my pregnancy.

Feeling confident that he could safely remove the baby, he said these life-changing words to us, "I can help you." What an incredible relief! Dr. Linzey *was* our answer to prayer! Tears filled my eyes as I sat there in awe. God had indeed provided a way!

Before we left his office, Dr. Linzey asked if he could pray with me and my husband. Listening to the comforting prayers of this amazing Christian doctor was such a stark contrast to the harsh experience with my first doctor. I knew with all my heart that God had orchestrated all the details.

As we thanked him, the doctor handed me copies of the ultrasound photos. To this day, these pictures are a reminder of God's faithfulness even when life did not go as we had hoped or planned.

Are you living in the middle of the unexpected? Has life's circumstances taken you off course without a way to move forward. God wants to help you. He truly does care. He sees you when you are hurting and loves to provide in ways beyond your wildest imagination!

Just like God provided for us when we could not see another way, I know that He can do the same for you.

Remember, you are not alone in your loss. God hears you and has not forgotten you. God is walking with you and providing what you need. This is wonderful news.

What do you need right now as you are experiencing loss? Have you prayed and asked God for help? Have you asked friends and family to come alongside you and pray for you?

Mark Batterson wrote an amazing book on prayer called *The*

Circle Maker. In it, he said, "The greatest tragedy in life is the prayers that go unanswered because they go unasked. 100 percent of the prayers I don't pray won't get answered."[3]

Mark encourages us to pray with persistence and continually circle our prayers, using the example of a man who drew a circle in the sand and did not budge until God answered his impossible prayer. We circle our prayers by never giving up and boldly bringing our overwhelming circumstances before the Lord and asking Him to intervene. Is there something specific you need to ask God to help you with? Maybe you need a friend, a doctor, or a monetary amount. Perhaps you need God's direction, wisdom, and guidance.

Don't give up. Keep praying! Fervently seek God in the middle of your heartbreaking circumstance. The most important part is the seeking. Mark says, "We shouldn't seek answers as much as we should seek God. If you seek answers, you won't find them, but if you seek God, the answers will find you."[4]

No wonder Matthew 7:7–8 tells us, *"Ask and it will be given to you; seek and you will find; knock and the door will be opened to you. For everyone who asks receives; the one who seeks finds; and to the one who knocks the door will be opened."*

As you surrender your heartbreak to God by seeking Him and asking Him for what you need, you will add intimacy and depth to your faith in Him. Sometimes what we need may be different from what we want. I know I get those mixed up at times. If you are not sure, I recommend praying for God to help you discern what you need versus what you want. I promise He will guide you.

Keep in mind, too, that God does not always answer our prayers when we want them answered. His timing is often slower than ours, and we have to wait longer than we want. God will provide what you need in the midst of the storm as you keep circling that prayer and diving deeper in your faith.

Let's Pray

> *God*, thank You for being my provider. Thank You for showing up when all hope is lost. I pray that I can remember to invite You into my difficult circumstances each day. I pray for Your strength, comfort, and wisdom. Guide me when I feel alone and forgotten. Remind me that you see me and hear me when I cry for help. Thank you for walking through this storm with me and growing my roots deeper in You. In Jesus's name, Amen.

Truth

> You are not alone in your loss. God hears you and has not forgotten you. God is walking with you and providing what you need.

Seek God and invite Him into your pain.

Tearfully allow yourself time to grieve and process the emotions.

Replace your finite view with God's infinite perspective.

Embrace God's character development in the midst of the chaos.

Never lose sight of God's grace.

Give praise to God even as your heart breaks.

Trust God is good when your mind is doubting and you don't understand.

Honestly share your story and help another hurting heart.

5

Facing the Emotions

A time to cry and a time to laugh.
A time to grieve and a time to dance.
Ecclesiastes 3:4 (NLT)

I wished I could take away all the pain.

Sitting silently across from Jeannie so as not to wake her from her third round of chemotherapy, the dreariness of the white, plain room lined with rows of recliner chairs devastated me. The light streaming in from the window and the view of the parking lot below could not add a trace of brightness to this desolate, quiet place. The only sounds were the footsteps of the nurses and the machines beeping as they released another round of treatment to the three patients, each with their own IV pole and drip bag.

Four recliners to my right, a young woman sat beside her loved one, who was wearing a beautiful headscarf to hide her hair loss. On the other side of the room, an old man rested alone with no one by his side. Glancing at him, sadness filled my heart. *I am so glad Jeannie's not alone.* I was thankful to be there to support my friend.

Jeannie struggled to stay asleep during the exhausting four-hour chemo session. As she napped, my mind drifted back to a special evening a few months earlier at Saddleback Church. Standing near the outdoor pool next to the children's ministry building, Jeannie and I clapped and cheered for our younger boys at the annual Kids Small Group (KSG) baptism celebration. The U-shaped amphitheater around the pool was packed with happy kids, parents, and grandparents watching the third grade KSG students, all in matching T-shirts, take their turns stepping into the water to be baptized. The crowd erupted with applause and excitement each time a child arose from the pool.

The children's pastor spoke individual words of encouragement to both Conor and Lucas, Jeannie's son, as they each made their public declaration of faith in the Lord. I love how God brings certain friends into our lives for a reason, knowing what the future holds. For Jeannie and me, God had purposely interweaved our paths so we could help each other through difficult times and create some amazing memories along the way. One of the greatest of those was being coleaders of KSG together alongside her daughter, Sophia. That joyful night at the KSG baptism, I snapped a picture of Jeannie with her husband and children, completely unaware of the cancer already growing inside of her and what the next months would bring.

Ping. The beep of the machine pumping drugs into Jeannie's frail body startled me back to reality—much the same way her shocking cancer diagnosis had startled me when she first told me about it. Honestly, her news left all of her family and friends on high alert.

Now, sitting with her in this clinic, I still struggled to make sense of it all. Jeannie was halfway through her six treatments and had already been to chemotherapy two times in just the last month. At her first chemo appointment, she had been talkative and full of life, befriending a man next to her and spreading joy to others.

However, this time was different. The cumulative effect of the drugs was taking its toll. Her body was restless. She was struggling to get comfortable in her chair. She even shared how her body ached in pain as she drifted in and out of sleep,

I knew my friend was fighting hard to battle her cancer. Hoping to stop its spread, the doctor had suggested a very aggressive approach; however, the treatment's side effects were just as aggressive. Jeannie was constantly sick to her stomach. Sometimes we wondered, *What is worse, the treatment or the cancer?*

After each round of chemo, it took about two weeks for Jeannie to feel like herself again, just in time for her to have to go in again for the next treatment. The side effects compounded each time, and Jeannie became weaker as she struggled to keep food down and continued to lose weight.

It was so hard to see her in such pain. I remember picking her up one day to drive her to another chemo appointment. I gasped as I saw the abrupt weight loss in her face. She looked like skin and bones. My heart sank. I was surprised at how quickly her body was deteriorating.

Storms can do this. Raging into your life, they can completely change its trajectory. Cancer is one of those violent storms. Thundering from out of nowhere, cancer can definitely turn your world upside down and leave you dealing with a gust of painful emotions.

I felt helpless to calm Jeannie's storm. Deep sadness overwhelmed my soul as I watched her suffering. Angry that she had to weather this storm, I was like a ball of pent-up frustration ready to burst.

What do you do when such hard emotions build up inside of you? How can you offer support to your loved one when you are exhausted from the storm? How do you deal with that grief in a healthy way when your life is not turning out how you hoped or planned?

Through years of talking with a counselor, I have learned that you have to walk through painful emotions in order to completely heal from them. My advice to you is to be completely honest about your hurt. Put a name to what you are feeling, and share it with someone you trust. Give yourself time to process and feel difficult emotions. The only way to begin to heal is to allow yourself time to feel.

When feelings are raw and the pain is too real, you might try to avoid your feelings, but Pastor Rick Warren accurately stated,

"If you don't let it out in healthy ways, you are going to act it out in unhealthy ways."[5]

Don't suppress the hurt and push it down deep as though it does not exist.

Don't numb the pain with alcohol or drugs, hoping it will disappear.

Don't escape the discomfort by distracting yourself from the reality of the situation. You will be tempted to keep busy by working longer hours or binge-watching television, but these responses will not help.

All of these methods will only prolong the agony and leave you feeling stuck.

You cannot go around your feelings. You have to go through them.

You cannot go around your feelings. You have to go through them. Only then are you able to process them and release them.

Here are some practical ways to process your emotions and take care of yourself when you are experiencing heartbreak.

Spend time with God.

Your ability to successfully deal with these hard emotions is directly proportional to the amount of time you spend with God. Let me encourage you to just hold on to God through it all. Lean in and share your heart with Him. Through prayer, studying your Bible, and reading devotionals, God will guide you along the path. Ask the Lord for energy and strength for each day, and allow God to fill you up with His love, comfort, and peace so you can pour all three into the life of your hurting loved one.

Surround yourself with people who care.

Stay connected with those who are understanding and will support you no matter what. This could be your family, friends, or your small group at church. Choose trustworthy people who will listen and encourage you. Find family members who can empathize and cry with you. Talk with loved ones who share your beliefs and can offer wisdom and advice. Be honest with how you are feeling and let others know what you need and how they can support you.

Journal your emotions.

Journaling is one of the ways that I just let out all of my raw emotions and really talk with God. It is extremely therapeutic for me. My pen gets writing, and I find it freeing to share the sadness, anger, disappointment, and *why* questions. To be completely honest, you will even find some swear words intermixed in my writing as I just pour out exactly how I am feeling—the good, the bad, and the ugly. I just write all of it. God can handle it. He wants to help you through the pain as you process your emotions.

Give it a try. Remember, there is no right or wrong way to journal. Just give yourself complete freedom to write the real, genuine emotions that you are feeling. Going back and reading my old journals has been faith building for me. Seeing examples of how God answered prayers ignites a fire within me. I can see time and again where God met me and guided me through the whole journey, every step of the way.

Talk with a therapist or professional counselor.

Talking with a professional counselor has been a huge part of my healing. As I sat on a couch pouring out my heart, she helped me identify and work through the many emotions from my heartbreaks. I found the "Feeling Words List" helpful, especially when I was struggling to put a name to how I felt. Her listening ear and helpful insights were instrumental in my recovery. I recommend meeting weekly with a counselor to help you process the emotions you are experiencing.

Join a support group.

Knowing others understand what you are going through will help in your healing. A support group is a great way to connect with others who are facing the same difficulties. Churches or community centers offer grief support groups centering on a specific need like cancer, divorce, infertility, or miscarriage. (I further discuss joining a group for added support in more detail in Chapter 7.)

Guard your heart and fill your mind with truth

Take a break from social media. For me, I needed to stop looking at Facebook for a short time. Social media can make you think that everyone has it all together and you are the only one whose life has been shattered. This was especially true for me during my divorce. Seeing pictures of families together reminded me that mine had fallen apart. Summer was especially tough because there were so many posts from happy couples celebrating their anniversaries. Each one felt like a dagger to my shattered heart. To protect yourself, take time away from social media.

A great way to fill your mind with God's truth is to listen to worship music. Songs are powerful and can put words to how you are feeling. If you find one that helps, listen to it repeatedly and let the lyrics flow over you. I remember lifting my hands in the air and just crying through certain songs.

In each of my heartbreaking circumstances, reading books played a huge part in my healing. Diving into their stories and hearing the authors validate what I was feeling helped me not feel alone. Knowing that someone understands you is important as you walk through grief. Books also gave me hope. As the writers shared how God brought them through their struggles, God whispered to me that He would guide me too. Books will not change your painful circumstances, but they can alter your perspective.

Practice self-care.

Dealing with difficult emotions will drain you physically and emotionally, so taking care of yourself is very important. Recharging with a good night's sleep is a necessity. Whenever possible, try your best to continue to eat a balanced diet and get some exercise so you don't end up run-down or sick.

I know that many times through a storm, you are giving to everyone else. Your loved ones need your support, extra time, and energy. If there are kids involved, you pour your love and time into them to help them process how they feel. Everyone needs so much from you that you can easily burn out because the emotional withdrawals are happening faster than the deposits.

Imagine you have a gauge like the fuel meter on your car. You can't afford to let yourself go empty. Therefore, find some ways to make deposits back into your life. What fills you up? Is it taking a walk to clear your head, a nap, a hot bath, reading, or journaling? I understand that you don't have big chunks of time to recharge, but sometimes just a little break or fresh air will help. Keep checking your gauge so you don't end up completely drained and out of gas. You know yourself best, so continue to fill up so you can pour out.

Give yourself time and grace.

You cannot rush your grief. Sadly, many people will want to hurry you along faster than you are ready, but you need to set your own pace. Don't worry about other people's expectations either. It is okay not to be okay. Give yourself lots of time and grace as you walk through your heartbreak.

Author Philip Yancey shares a scuba diving analogy when he speaks on grief.[6] He describes it as being underwater. Most people want to get you up to the surface as fast as possible, but it is not safe to ascend too quickly. Scuba divers know there are safety stops at certain depths where they need to wait and breathe to equalize their pressure. When someone is experiencing loss and grief, they need loved ones to wait submerged underwater with them until they are ready to come up to the next level.

Grief will take longer than you expect. Take the time to feel all the emotions at each level before rising to the next stop. "Grief is the place where love and pain converge,"[7] Yancey said. Remember, all the tears and sadness are evidence of how much you deeply cared and loved.

Let's Pray

> *God,* help me process my emotions in a healthy way. Please guide me in finding a Christian counselor or godly friend to share all that I am feeling. I know it is easier to suppress the hard emotions or try to escape the pain, but God, I pray you will empower me to be brave enough to walk through it. I want to allow myself time to feel so that I can begin to heal. God, help me journal my thoughts and feelings to You daily. Guard my heart and mind so I can stay focused on You through the grief. In Jesus's name, Amen.

Truth

> The only way to begin to heal is to allow yourself time to feel.

6

The Power of Words

*Therefore encourage one another
and build each other up.*
1 Thessalonians 5:11

I wished I had different words to say.

My son, Conor, sped past me on his bike at the park directly across the street from our house. Happy and carefree, he smiled ear to ear as his older brother, Kyle, rode right behind him, chasing him on the giant sidewalk loop around the grass. It was always a joy to see them having fun together. Untroubled and unaware of the weight of the world, they giggled and laughed.

But not me. I knew that everything was about to change.

The sun was shining bright that Friday afternoon, but nothing in my heart felt warm or cheerful. Instead, my stomach was in knots just thinking about the conversation my husband and I needed to have with our boys. My stress intensified each time my kids zoomed past me. *How do I tell them their dad will no longer be living at our house? It is going is to break their hearts.*

There were good days in my children's lives that I knew they would never forget, like the first time Kyle rode Space Mountain at

Disneyland or the day Conor won the championship hockey game. However, this was not one of those days. In my heart, I knew they would never forget the day their family fell apart, the day their parents told them they were splitting up.

My heart kept beating faster each time the boys wheeled past me. My palms were sweaty, and I was a nervous wreck. Just then, their dad's car pulled up to the side of the house. The time had come to tell them the life-changing news together.

"Kyle! Conor!" I hollered. "Your dad is here." Quickly, they pedaled their bikes across the street to greet their father. Excited to see him, they jumped up and down, completely unaware that their reality was about to be flipped upside down. With shaky hands, I opened the front door, and we all entered the house as a family one last time.

With all four of us facing each other on the L-shaped couch in the living room, we told them the news. My youngest son immediately burst into tears and fell into my arms. I held him tightly as my head rested down on his. Only a first grader, Conor's heart was breaking right before my eyes, and I could not take the pain away. My older fifth grade son had a vastly different response. Sitting stoically and completely still, there were no tears, no response at all—just silence. I leaned toward Kyle, pulled him close to me, and hugged him.

I thought to myself, *We are completely screwing up our kids. One day, they will be in counseling sharing this day with their therapist.* With a heavy heart and tears rolling down my face, I embraced my boys and prayed for them.

Have you ever had to share something that left your family in tears? Maybe it was a health diagnosis or news about a job loss. Perhaps it was more somber, like a death in the family. No matter what the reason, life-shattering words can leave us feeling a mixture of emotions such as shock, sadness, and anger. Together, they produce the grief we feel after experiencing loss.

Grief comes in waves. At the beginning, my waves crashed quickly and regularly. Suddenly, I was a single mom trying to help my kids while at the same time needing to grieve. Sometimes I could barely get through one wave before another one would come smashing down.

I was in survival mode.

Gasping for air.

Struggling to keep my head above water.

Trying to comfort my hurting children at the same time as I was dealing with the greatest heartbreak of my life.

Grief is challenging whatever its cause. It's a death—of a loved one, of a marriage, of a dream, of hope. Our hearts need time to process the emotions and begin to heal. We need family and friends who can come alongside us and offer empathy, words of encouragement, and support.

At a funeral, family members gather and celebrate their loved one by sharing stories and memories. They cry, say their goodbyes, and grieve as one. Even though these occasions can be extremely hard, I believe they serve a greater purpose. They allow people to experience grief together.

But what do you do when there is a death without a funeral?

What do you do when your final in vitro procedure does not work, and your dreams of giving birth to a baby pass away?

What do you do when the person you thought was going to love you forever says they don't love you anymore?

Infertility is the death of the hopes and dreams for a family. Divorce is the death of a marriage. There is no funeral for infertility, no memorial service for a divorce. Loved ones do not gather to grieve. They do not celebrate the memories you shared or your hopes for the future.

Jason Gray wrote a song called "Death Without a Funeral" as he was going through a divorce. He said, "'Death Without a Funeral' was in essence my funeral service for something I love very much, which was my family." When asked to share the meaning behind his song, he revealed, "Grieving a divorce is difficult. If a loved one dies, there is a funeral or service where you say good-bye and have closure, friends gather around you, and you have a moment. When a divorce happens, I think sometimes friends do not know what to do and there are not clear ending markers, so it makes grief complicated. This makes healing complicated."[8]

For those of us who have gone through a divorce, Jason's song is particularly powerful. He eloquently puts into words what so many feel. Grieving alone, the pain and loss are just as real as if someone physically died. In addition, there is usually a layer of rejection attached to it. A friend of mine who was in the middle of a divorce shared that it would have been easier for her heart to grieve his loss if he had died rather than to grieve his choice to leave her for another woman. Feelings of betrayal were added to her grief, compounding her pain even more.

Multiplying the grief is the fact that if you have children together, you still must co-parent with the person who deeply hurt you. You have no choice but to see them as you exchange the kids back and forth. This makes healing exceedingly difficult.

Finally, like Jason said, friends and family do not always know what to say when you are going through a divorce. I agree, and I would add that most people do not know what to say to someone experiencing any kind of grief. Sometimes they say insensitive things. Other times, they say nothing at all. The absence of words can be just as unkind as saying the wrong ones.

Words are powerful, so let me share some helpful statements to say as well as hurtful ones to avoid. I have compiled everything I have learned from therapy I have experienced, books I have read, and videos I have watched. I want to share with you the four ways people can respond to your emotions and what they might say.

1. Fix your emotions.	"You just need to do X, Y, and Z, and then you will be better."
2. Minimize your emotions	"That is nothing. You should hear what I am going through. It is much worse."
3. *"Silver line" your emotions.	*At least* you know you can still get pregnant"[9] (when you share with someone about your miscarriage). *At least*, you did not get pancreatic cancer, I have heard that is much worse" (when you tell a family member about your breast cancer diagnosis).
4. Empathize with your emotions.	"That must be hard. I am so sorry. I am here for you."

*Brené Brown has an excellent YouTube video I recommend on empathy vs. sympathy. She introduced me to this term, "silver lining" your emotions and it involves using the words, "At least." In addition to the examples above, here are some more: You confide with a friend that you are having marriage struggles, and they say, "At least you are married."[10] You share with your small group that your son has been home sick for three days, and they say, "At least your daughter is healthy." Those words, "At least" do not help you connect with the true pain your loved one is feeling. As you are trying to make them feel better, you are actually missing a moment to show empathy and offer understanding.

After reading these examples, I hope it is obvious that your goal should be empathy!

So, what can you say and what should you avoid?

Here are some words that I found helpful:

- "I am so sorry you are going through this. How can I pray for you?"

- "How can I help you? Let me know if there is anything you need."

- "Tell me more. I am here for you whenever you need someone to listen."

- "It is okay not to be okay. Take all the time you need to grieve and heal."

Your words will let them know that you care and are ready and available to walk through this storm with them.

These statements validate the hurt and show that you want to understand what they are feeling. Your words will let them know that you care and are ready and available to walk through this storm with them.

In addition to the fixing, minimizing, and silver-lining words, I also recommend avoiding these words:

- "Everything is going to be fine." This statement shows a lack of empathy because their entire life has just changed, and it does not feel fine.

- "Just move on. You are better off without them." This could be true, but in the middle of the pain, no one wants to hear this. Remember, this person's heart has been broken into a million tiny pieces, and they are deeply hurting.

- "This is a blessing in disguise," or "Everything happens for a reason." Both of these statements are attempts to sugarcoat the situation to make the person feel better. Instead, try putting yourself in their shoes and enter into the pain they are feeling.

- "God is more interested in your character than your comfort." Again, this is a true statement—but timing is especially important. Maybe you can share advice like this once they are farther along in their grief, but saying this immediately is not helpful.

These lists are intended to start the conversation. Perhaps there are other words you would add to each list. I recommend sharing with your loved ones the words you want them to share with you in your grief, words that will build you up instead of tear you down.

To encourage a friend who was having a hard day, Holley Gerth wrote these words in her book *Under God's Umbrella.*

> I wish I had a big yellow umbrella
> that would keep away all the rain in your life.
> I would hold it over your head,
> and the drops would splash, splash,
> and you would never even feel them.
> But I don't have a big yellow umbrella,
> so I'll walk through the rain with you.[11]

The words show such love and comfort to someone who is hurting. They expressed Holley's desire to connect with that person in the middle of their storm. Everyone wants to be heard and understood. Everyone desires empathy. No one needs quick solutions to their problems or comparisons to others with greater issues. No one wants to try to find the silver lining in their pain. All of these attempts to help will actually cause the other person to pull away.

It is only when you identify with the hard emotions of others that you will truly connect with them. Empathy is a gift you offer through listening, understanding, and connecting to someone in their hurt or pain.

The causes of our heartbreak may be different, but the whirlwind of difficult emotions is universal. We all need loved ones willing to walk through the storm with us and even to hold the umbrella for us.

Let's Pray

> *God*, thank You for family and friends who encourage and support me in the middle of my heartbreaking emotions. I know there is power in words, so I pray today for empathy and grace in how I respond to those who are hurting and in how they respond to me and my pain. Empower me to listen more than talk, to not try to minimize or fix, but really lean in, connect, and give the gift of complete presence. God, help us walk through the storm with others showing love, understanding, and empathy. In Jesus's name, Amen.

Truth

> Empathy is a gift you offer through listening, understanding, and connecting to someone in their hurt or pain.

7

Empty Arms

Blessed are those who mourn,
for they will be comforted.
Matthew 5:4

I was not ready to say goodbye.

That Sunday evening, I smiled as I spotted the two familiar cars in the church parking lot. Each represented grieving parents who had lost a baby, people who supported and encouraged me in my greatest time of need following my loss. Ironically, the nearly empty church parking lot mirrored our empty arms. Parking between these cars for the eighth week in a row, my heart was conflicted. It was the final week of our support group.

Living through the past two months had been like walking through a heavy haze. It was hard to see any light through the constant cloud of grief. One of the hardest moments was right after my miscarriage when I shared the sad news with my three-year-old son, Kyle. As I drove from the long, tiring doctor's appointment to my parent's house where they babysat him, a weightiness overcame my heart. *How do you explain death to a three-year-old?* I had no idea what I was going to say.

As I opened the door, my energetic toddler ran into my arms. Excited to be a big brother, he hugged and kissed my belly. I immediately knelt on the carpet with him so we could be face-to-face. My red, puffy eyes unmasked the fact that I had been bawling.

With a concerned look, Kyle asked, "What's wrong, Mommy?"

I gave him the biggest hug and told him the baby had stopped growing and was now in heaven. He just held me tight, and together we cried and embraced in the middle of the living room.

Tears became a regular part of our daily life that summer. With the whirlwind of emotions, I was often at a loss about how to deal with them. Normally, I would love to go on playdates and be around people, but the miscarriage changed me. One day, knowing I needed to get my rambunctious boy out of the house, I mustered up the energy to go to a bookstore. Kyle couldn't wait to play at the Thomas the Train table.

As he was zooming the train cars around the track, another mom and her son approached. Trying to make small talk, she asked, "Do you have any other children?"

I was speechless. *How can I answer that question? In one sense, my baby never took her first breath here on earth, but on the other hand, she was still one of my children.* Tearing up, I flustered my words as I attempted to share that I had recently miscarried my second child.

It was in moments like those that I was so thankful for our Sunday night support group.

Not only did they listen to my struggles and help me process my feelings, they also helped me troubleshoot situations like the one at the bookstore. Together, we prepared an answer to the woman's question that had left me rattled. I learned to say with ease, "I have one child here on earth and one child up in heaven."

The Empty Arms Support Group reminded me that I was not experiencing my grief alone. By honestly sharing our emotions and processing everything we had experienced during and since our losses, this group was a comfort in the middle of our chaos. One Sunday evening, we discussed hurtful words people had said to us. I shared an insensitive comment a mom said to me. Trying to explain why my baby had stopped growing, she said it was nature's way of selecting who should live or not. She even used the words "survival of the fittest." Being able to safely share those upsetting words and talk about them in our group brought healing.

As I walked from the parking lot toward the church, I could not believe it was already the final night of class. In my heart, I knew I was going to miss the group who had been such a gift in my grief.

As our final task that night, we each wrote a letter to our babies. I found it to be incredibly therapeutic, and I recommend it to you if you are grieving a child you never knew. In it, share the hopes and dreams you had for your baby, and be honest about your loss. That's exactly what I did. I closed my letter with these words: "Although you never got to experience life here on earth, you will always be remembered in my heart! Love, Mom."

In what ways is your heart breaking over the loss of a loved one? What can you do to keep the waves of grief from knocking you down as you try to move forward? How can you deepen your faith even as you question why God would allow this to happen?

Grief is the natural response to loss. Like the uniqueness of a snowflake, no one will deal with it exactly the same as another. Even though everyone grieves differently, psychologist Dr. Elisabeth Kubler-Ross identified five stages of grief. At Empty Arms we learned about the stages: denial, anger, bargaining, depression, and acceptance.

Like the uniqueness of a snowflake, no one will deal with grief exactly the same.

Grieving is more like a roller coaster than a straight line. It is full of twists and turns. It is likely you will not go through each stage in this exact order either. You will bounce back and forth between stages as you allow yourself time to process your emotions.

Let's break down each step further.

Denial

This is the stage of grief when you are thinking, *This cannot be happening to me.* The shock of your loss has left you numb and overwhelmed. Like a defense mechanism, denial helps you cope with the life-altering news. Because you can only deal with so much at once, denial allows you to pace your feelings. I like what David Kessler says about denial: "There is a grace in denial. It is nature's way of letting in only as much as we can handle."[12]

Anger

As your denial starts to fade, you are left with hard emotions. As these feelings surface, you will begin to feel anger as you try to make sense of it all. Underlying your anger is the pain from the loss of your loved one. You are thinking, *Why did this happen to me?* Because you are trying to process the hurt, you want to find someone to blame: your doctor, your spouse, yourself, and many times, God. You ask, *Where was God* or *Why, Lord* during this stage of grief. Don't attempt to suppress your anger. It is part of the grief cycle and a necessary step.

Bargaining

Striving to take back some control, you try to bargain or plead with God. "Please, God, I promise to live a better life if you will let my loved one live. Lord, I will devote the rest of my life to helping others if you bring my loved one back." Feeling guilty is common in this stage of grief. You encounter the what-if and if-only statements. You say, "If only we had gone to the doctor sooner" or "What if we had got a second opinion?" Because you want to cope, you think of what you could have done differently.

Depression

As you gradually return to the present reality, you come face-to-face with the difficult emotions surrounding your loss, and your grief goes to a deeper level. Intense sadness, emptiness, and withdrawing from others are parts of this stage in the grief cycle. Because you think it is going to last forever, you may not want to get out of bed in the morning. According to Kessler, "Depression is the appropriate response to a great loss."[13] Feeling hopeless, it is like you are living in a fog. You need to allow yourself time to process these real and raw emotions.

Acceptance

In this stage of grief, you still feel the pain from your loss, but you have come to accept the reality of it. I like Kubler-Ross's example of acceptance. She says, "Not in the sense that 'it's okay my husband died,' rather 'my husband died, but I'm going to be okay.'"[14] This does not mean you are completely over it and you will not have another hard day. That is a common misconception. You will never be completely over your loss. However, in this stage, the good days are starting to outnumber the bad ones.

As you go through these steps, remember that you cannot rush grief. It is not something you do once and never do again. It is a process commonly referred to as waves. At the beginning, they hit you one right after another. But over time, the waves become further apart.

Pastor Levi Lusko explains grief in a way I had never heard before in his book *Through the Eyes of a Lion*. He experienced the unthinkable when his five-year-old daughter died of an asthma attack in his arms. He describes grief as reverse pregnancy. The very last stage of childbirth is when the baby is crowning, and it is referred to as the ring of fire. According to Levi, this is where grief begins, right at most immense pain and hurt. He wrote, "You don't work up to the worst—you start there, gripped by spasms of agony so fierce you cry out gutturally and come physically undone."[15]

From there, Levi goes backward in the delivery to the contractions. "From the ring of fire, you transition into heavy sorrow. The contractions of sadness start out so stacked together, so constant, that it feels like an unending seizure of suffering. As the days give way to weeks, there are moments of respite between these attacks as you learn to breathe and ride them out."[16] Unlike pregnancy, the pain will never completely go away with grief. It will just subside with time.

This is a powerful illustration of grief. As you experience the ring of fire and heavy sorrow, you will need support from others. Grieving is a difficult process, so please don't walk through the intense hurt alone. Search for a grief support group in your area. Surround yourself with people who are not going to rush you or minimize what you are going through. Find strength from others who are walking through a similar heartbreak, and together you can help each other through the pain.

Our Sunday night Empty Arms Support Group was a blessing in the middle of our grief. Even though I was still heartbroken over the loss of my baby, I saw how valuable it was to have a safe place to share each week. Walking through grief is hard, but walking through grief with no support is even harder. Don't forget—you were never meant to grieve alone.

Let's Pray

> *God*, help me find a strong support group to encourage me during my time of grief. Guide me to find people who can listen and empathize with me as I face my hard emotions. Allow me to find strength from others who have walked this path before and can offer comfort and understanding. Thank You for Your love, comfort, and strength in the middle of this unexpected storm. Continue to grow my faith deeper in you. In Jesus's name, Amen.

Truth

Attending a grief support group provides you with comfort, understanding, and strength from others who have walked the path before you. You were never meant to grieve alone.

<u>S</u>eek God and invite Him into your pain.

<u>T</u>earfully allow yourself time to grieve and process the emotions.

<u>R</u>eplace your finite view with God's infinite perspective.

<u>E</u>mbrace God's character development in the midst of the chaos.

<u>N</u>ever lose sight of God's grace.

<u>G</u>ive praise to God even as your heart breaks.

<u>T</u>rust God is good when your mind is doubting and you don't understand.

<u>H</u>onestly share your story and help another hurting heart.

8

The Smallest Details

Cast your cares on the Lord
and he will sustain you.
Psalm 55:22

I was completely in awe.

With my cell phone in one hand and my dog's leash in the other, I raced across the street to the park. Excited we were taking another walk, Shadow, my 110-pound black Lab, pulled me along the sidewalk circle that surrounded the large, green grass field. This same loop that my kids rode their bikes on just a month before had become my safe haven, a place where I could freely talk and honestly share with friends how I was feeling.

Oh, if that park had ears, it would have heard it all: tears, frustrations, heartbreak, and disappointment.

The bright morning sun shone directly in my eyes as if it was trying to sprinkle some light and hope into my dark, challenging days. Lack of sleep. Exhaustion. More questions than I had answers. I was barely surviving the waves of grief from the end of my marriage. Add my kids' grief to the mix, and truthfully, it was more than I could handle.

Escaping to the park to share my latest struggle with friends had become part of my survival routine. In addition to counseling once a week, processing my emotions with loved ones brought new life in the middle of my devastating circumstances. I dialed my friend's number as Shadow and I took our third walk that morning. Honestly, I think the dog was the only one who liked the new arrangement. The rest of us were really struggling.

As she answered the phone, I blurted out, "My niece is getting married! A special invitation just arrived in the mail."

What previously would have been exciting news suddenly made me anxious. "I have never driven this far by myself," I told my friend. "What if I get sleepy on the way there? Where will I stay when I get there? I have always stayed with my in-laws, but that is no longer an option." Each worry out of my mouth increased my blood pressure about taking this four-hour trip alone. My friend listened patiently as I freaked out.

The thought of missing my niece's wedding made my cry, but the thought of taking this emotional trip alone made my cry even harder. I was a hot mess.

Thankfully, my friend interrupted my meltdown and suggested that I call some friends who had relatives in the same area to see if they could accompany me on the trip. I made a list with only three names. Praying one of them could help, I dialed my closest friend of the trio whose in-laws lived about an hour away. Sadly, they were coming down to visit her that same weekend. Crossing her name off the list, I moved to the next friend whose sister lived close by. Unfortunately, she shared that she was traveling up north to visit her the following weekend and could not do both.

Miss Jackie, my sons' Mommy and Me preschool teacher, was the final name on the list. We exchanged holiday cards every year, but it had been years since my sons had her as a teacher. Her sister lived in the same town as my in-laws, but I debated calling her because of the long span of time since we had last spoken. Knowing in my heart that I should not take the road trip on my own, I decided to reach out to her.

Little did I know that God was already working out all the specifics.

On Wednesday morning, I was driving in my car by myself. If you have kids, you know that alone time in the car is rare and precious. With no distractions from my little ones, I got ready to call Miss Jackie. But as I searched for her name on my cell phone, I realized her number was only on my Christmas card list at home on my computer. My call would have to wait until the next day.

Thursday morning, I found her number and quickly punched it in. Surprised to get a wrong number, I checked it again and realized I had misdialed it. *That was odd*, I thought. I tried again with the correct number, but the call went to voice mail. I left Miss Jackie a message to call back when she got a chance because I had something to ask her.

Now, you may be wondering why I am going into so much detail on when and how I called her. They seem unimportant—but I'd soon learn they were anything but that. God was showing up in the small details.

Friday, Jackie returned my call. I updated her on my predicament and inquired about her driving up north with me. With no plans to visit her sister that weekend, she needed to check her calendar and get back to me. In my heart, I knew it didn't look promising. As I hung up the phone, tears started flowing down my face. Knowing she was the last person on my list, I assumed that I would probably have to make the trip alone.

Alone. This word was becoming all too familiar.

Trying to convince myself that I would be okay, I began to mentally prepare myself.

Two days later, my phone rang. It was Miss Jackie. "I can drive up with you!" Her excitement was contagious, but I was surprised by her words. Taken aback, I apologized for bugging her with something so small and began to tell her it was okay for her to back out.

She interrupted me mid-sentence. "Jodi, I need to tell you something. I was planning to tell you on the drive up, but I think you need to hear it now." She had my full attention.

"When you first called me on Thursday, I was at Bible study. Our group was talking about how God brings different people into our lives for different seasons, and he brought your name to mind. I shared with the group how we met through Mommy and Me—and right after I was done talking, my phone rang."

I had called her at the *exact* moment God had placed my name in her mind.

If I had reached her on Wednesday morning as I had first planned when I was alone in the car, it would have been too soon. If I had not misdialed her number on Thursday morning, I would have been calling minutes too early. God was working everything out.

Speechless, I listened to her words. I could not believe it. God had placed me on her heart even before she knew I needed help. I was stunned by God's perfect timing. With fresh tears in my eyes, I sat there amazed that the God of the universe cared that much about me.

Jackie continued, "I feel very strongly that God wants me to take this trip with you. I have cleared my calendar for the entire weekend and can leave whenever you want to go." Completely shocked and encouraged by her words, I started to sob.

Up until this point, I knew God cared about me, but I thought it was only about the big issues in life: who to marry, what job to take, where to live. But hearing that God knew about the little details that were causing me worry and that He would orchestrate all of it for me, I felt His immense love. I was completely in awe of Him.

Surprisingly, He still wasn't done yet. Before she hung up the phone, Jackie inquired, "Do you have a place to stay when you get there?" I told her I didn't. "Would you like to stay at my sister's house?" Again, I wept at God's provision for me. I'd had moments where I felt God's presence before, but now I was confident that He was always with me every step of the way.

Friend, God is with you every step of the way too. He cares deeply about the little details in your life. He sees you and has not forgotten you. He wants to help you through your hard circumstances.

Looking back now, that trip was an important step in my journey. You see, the confidence I got from driving those four hours up north with Jackie would then give me the confidence to take my boys on a road trip that summer, but that is a story for another chapter.

Unexpectedly, the drive with Jackie was super easy. I did not get tired or feel incapable at all while going there or driving home. In fact, I remember saying to her on the way back, "I don't know why I was so worried about this."

My heart was so thankful to Jackie for being there with me and walking (or should I say, driving) through it with me. God knew that I should not be alone on the trip, and I love that He made sure to provide a strong Christian woman to accompany me. We talked about our faith and how God is working in our lives, especially in the hard times, the whole ride up.

My niece's wedding was beautiful. Even though it was hard on me emotionally, I was thrilled to be there to support her on her special day. It turned out the wedding was the last family event I attended on my husband's side of the family. It was hard to say goodbye and give hugs knowing that things would never be the same. I was no longer going to be part of their family like I was before. This is one of the saddest parts of the divorce for me. Even now, I still miss my relationships with my nieces, nephews, and in-laws.

That God-orchestrated road trip taught me so many important lessons about the Lord.

First, God genuinely cares about all your needs, from the big ones on down. It's easy to think of God providing for the big things in life, but when He shows up in the smallest of details, it becomes so clear just how much God truly loves you.

It's in the details where God reminds you that He is there, helping you through your difficult times.

It takes looking back on your circumstances to see God's hand over all of them.

Second, God sees you and has not forgotten you. As you go through hardship or grief, it is important to remember that God knows the hurt and pain that you are feeling and wants to provide people in your life to help you go through them. It is easy to see only the negative, but it takes looking back on your circumstances to see God's hand over all of them. Let me encourage you, as you are walking through your storm, to stop and see how God is providing for you.

This reminds me of the lyrics from a favorite worship song, "Waymaker." Allow me to summarize them for you: Sometimes we cannot see or feel God working, but He still is.

I am so thankful that God never stops working behind the scenes for us.

Last, God wants to use you to help others. As I write this story, I realize that Jackie could have said, *I don't want to inconvenience myself and go on this four-hour road trip and give up my whole weekend.* The outcome would have been completely different if she had not allowed God to use her to help me. This got me thinking about people in my life that God has placed on my mind. Is there someone in your life that you need to be there for and help, like Jackie did for me?

If you are going through a hard time, let me remind you to look for God in the details. I hope you experience your own in-awe-of-God moment.

Let's Pray

God, thank You that you are working behind the scenes even when I cannot see it. I pray that You will remind me each day that You see me and hear me, especially when I feel forgotten. Bring people into my life who will walk alongside me and help me through the pain. Thank You for showing up in the details and providing for me. I am in awe of You! In Jesus's name, Amen."

Truth

Replace your thoughts that God has forgotten you with the truth that God sees you and cares about even the smallest details.

9

Cracked Pot

We now have this light shining in our hearts,
but we ourselves are like fragile clay jars
containing this great treasure.
This makes it clear that our great power
is from God, not from ourselves.
We are pressed on every side by troubles,
but we are not crushed.
We are perplexed, but not driven to despair.
We are hunted down, but never abandoned by God.
We get knocked down, but we are not destroyed.
2 Corinthians 4:7–9 NLT

I could not believe what God revealed to me.

Boom! Crack!

I wonder if the neighbors heard that, I thought as I stared at the pile of broken pottery pieces on the ground.

That Saturday morning, my backyard had become an experiment ground. My mission was to purposefully break a clay pot and glue the pieces back together. Little did I know that God was about to expand my view on brokenness.

The idea came from Suzie Eller's book *The Mended Heart: God's*

Healing for Your Broken Places. Reading it the night before, I was fascinated by Suzie's account of her friend who sadly had walked through a broken relationship. What intrigued me the most was what that woman held up to the audience as she shared her story.

Suzie wrote that her friend "stills sees herself as broken, but she no longer feels like her life has been shattered. Rather, she is like a mosaic with a Light shining from the inside out. In fact, when she shares her testimony, she holds up a clay pot, broken and glued back together, for the audience to see. It's not perfect—or even beautiful by most human standards—but the Light filtering through the cracks is."[17]

I pondered, *I never thought something broken could be beautiful.*

Captivated by that lovely illustration of light glistening its way through the cracks in her clay pot, I just knew I needed to discover how that looked and felt for myself.

Broken—I could relate to that. The shattered dreams and smashed hopes of my own life resembled those broken pieces. The first time my heart cracked like a clay pot, I was staring at the ultrasound monitor and could not find my baby's heartbeat. I felt crushed, destroyed. The next time my heart was shattered was my devastating divorce. I felt damaged, wrecked. The most recent heartbreak was holding my dearest friend's hand through chemotherapy but still losing her to cancer only four months later. I felt fractured, ruined.

Each moment had left me splintered and beaten down by the weight of my grief. *How can I piece the fragments back together?* I honestly was not sure, but after reading about the broken pot in Suzie's book, I was hopeful. Perhaps there was a purpose to my brokenness.

Maybe you are wondering the same thing.

What if God's light shines the brightest through our cracks and broken places?

You see, a pot with no cracks or chips does not allow much light through it. However, if a pot has many of those broken places but still shines brightly for Jesus despite them, then that is a beautiful thing.

Could our brokenness actually help us be a stronger light?

Friend, there is power in doing something physically that symbolizes how you feel emotionally. I discovered this truth when I broke my own piece of pottery that weekend in my backyard. What God revealed to me unleashed hope.

Maybe you don't see hope as you are raising your kids as a single parent. Perhaps you feel hopeless watching your child make another poor choice, such as getting caught up in a drug or alcohol addiction. It could be that you don't see hope as you stare at another negative pregnancy test or drive to another chemo appointment.

Hope is an important ingredient as we look at our broken pieces.

After I had grabbed a hammer and headed to my backyard with a piece of pottery, I discovered how purposely breaking the pot so that I could glue the pieces back together was harder than I thought. I did not want to completely shatter it. Realizing the hammer would likely demolish it too much, I picked up the pottery and hit it against the concrete flowerbed. *Boom!* Nothing happened. Astonished, I tried again a little harder. *Pop!* A tiny splinter appeared. The ceramic art became easier to crack. In no time, the entire pot broke into pieces.

As I gathered up all the pieces to glue the pot back together, I noticed that there were small pieces, and even some dust, that came off with the cracks that I could not restore. What do we do with the dust? What happens to the small pieces that are lost? I love what Lysa TerKeurst shares about dust in her book *It's Not Supposed To Be This Way*. She says, "But what about those times when things aren't just broken but shattered beyond repair? Shattered to the point of dust. At least when things are broken there's some hope you can glue the pieces back together. But what if there aren't even pieces to pick up in front of you! You can't glue dust."[18]

Maybe as you look at your life, you just see dust. You feel shattered and broken beyond repair. I want to offer you hope. Lysa continues, "Dust is the exact ingredient God loves to use."[19] She reminds us that in the beginning, God formed man out of the dust. God breathed life into it, and Adam was formed.

She also shared the biblical story of the blind man whose eyesight Jesus restored by spitting into the dust and placing it over the man's eyes. "When mixed with water, dust becomes clay. Clay, when placed in the potter's hands, can be formed into anything the potter dreams up! Dust doesn't have to signify the end. Dust is often what must be present for the new to begin."[20]

This provides great perspective as you look at the dust from your broken life. Is your breaking actually the remaking of you? A more patient you? A more empathetic you? A *deeper* you?

As I looked at the dust and small broken pieces on the ground in my backyard, I realized that the pot can never be fully restored back to its original form. We will never be completely the same again after we break. I used to think that this was a bad thing, but now I have a different mindset.

What if we are not supposed to look exactly the same? What if we are becoming a better version of ourselves through our hard times? Brokenness changes us for the better when we allow God to breathe life into our dust.

I was in awe of what God was teaching me through my cracked pot. When it was time to piece together the broken fragments. I plugged in my hot glue gun and put the remains of the pottery back together. As I placed a candle inside the reassembled pot, I was surprised by what I saw.

The beams of light were shining radiantly through the slivers and cracks in the clay. It was breathtaking! That night, I took many pictures to remind me that God can take my broken pieces and turn them into something beautiful—and that He will do the same for you.

Let me say it again: God wants to take your broken pieces and turn them into something beautiful. Just imagine others seeing God's light shine brightly through the cracks and hard times of your life! That light is appealing, and it will invite them to be vulnerable and share their own broken stories.

There is beauty in brokenness.

Have you ever heard of *kintsugi*? It is a Japanese art where the artist intentionally uses broken pieces of pottery. Instead of trying to hide their brokenness, the artist highlights each crack with a gold lacquer, making the pot more valuable with each fracture. After all the holes have been redeemed, the finished product is a treasure.

The *kintsugi* clay pot is priceless, not in spite of its cracks but because of them.

So are you! God takes your broken heart and pieces it back together. He takes your broken story and turns it into a redemption story.

Are you ready for your mess to become your message? Do you want God to bring beauty to your ashes? Your broken story is a gift to share with others.

Let me share a story with you about two pots.

> Each day, a woman used two pots to collect water from a stream. As she walked back to her house, the first pot, perfect in every way, felt proud that it never leaked a drop of water. The second pot, with its multiple cracks and broken places, felt ashamed from always losing more than half of the water along the path. No matter how hard it tried, it felt like it never measured up to the other pot.
>
> One day, the pots overheard the woman talking with her neighbor. She asked, "What's your secret for the lovely flowers along the path?" The woman shared, "I sprinkled seeds knowing one of my pots is broken. Each day, the cracked pot spills water and helps these seeds grow. What was once a barren path is now filled with gorgeous flowers."[21]

I love that the second pot, with all its cracks and breaks, is the one that helps others grow. I think we believe just the opposite. We feel we need to have it all together to help someone else. But what if our hurt and pain is the very thing that qualifies us?

If I am honest, sometimes I want to be like the first pot, perfect in every way. Maybe you have struggled with perfectionism too. But I realize that the second pot, the broken one, helps others more. People will better relate to us through our brokenness than in our perfection. Friend, you will connect with others more in your struggles than you ever could with your successes.

You will connect with others more in your struggles than you ever could with your successes.

I used to think that our brokenness disqualified us, but now I know it is the very ingredient God uses to help another hurting heart. I love that God wants to use us because of our brokenness, not in spite of it.

Have you ever thought of your brokenness as a gift? Have you ever considered that God can take your brokenness and bring new growth in others from it?

Replace your fear that your brokenness disqualifies you with the truth that your brokenness qualifies you even more.

I am so thankful for the truth God revealed to me about brokenness that weekend. God wants to shine the brightest through our broken places. But are you willing to give Him your broken pieces? Allow God to take them and turn them into something wonderful. Your trials can be your testimony.

Remember, your brokenness does not have to define you. In God's hands, it can refine you into something stronger and more beautiful than ever before.

Let's Pray

God, I love that You don't waste our broken pieces. Thank You for redeeming them and using them to comfort another hurting heart. Keep reminding me that my brokenness does not disqualify me. Show me someone who needs encouragement, and give me the courage to share my broken story with them. I want to be a beacon of light and hope. God, help me shine brighter than I ever have before! In Jesus's name, Amen.

Truth

Replace your fear that your brokenness disqualifies you with the truth that your brokenness qualifies you even more.

10

The Bigger Picture

I am not saying this because I am in need,
for I have learned to be content whatever
the circumstances. I know what it is to be in need,
and I know what it is to have plenty.
I have learned the secret of being content
in any and every situation, whether well fed or hungry,
whether living in plenty or in want.
I can do all this through him who gives me strength.
Philippians 4:11–13

I wished the circumstances were different.

I called to the kids, "It's time to load the car!" They excitedly followed me out the door, each of us rolling a suitcase. I lifted each heavy bag into the back of the vehicle, and I was surprised by the weightlessness I felt in my own heart about the trip. Visiting friends along the scenic ocean drive to San Francisco was just what we needed.

As I closed the trunk, my mind drifted back to our last family vacation. Just six months ago, all four of us explored the beautiful island of Kauai, snorkeling together and hiking to a waterfall—all together. Sadly, our life had drastically changed in the half year since the divorce got under way.

Together looked different now. As the boys skipped to the car and jumped into the back seat, I opened the door to the driver's side and settled in. I was ready to begin our first summer vacation as a family of three.

As I put the keys in the starter, I recalled a conversation I had with my lawyer just two months before. Distraught over not having my kids with me for Easter break, I sobbed when he asked the ages of my boys. Embarrassment came over me at my failure to keep myself together emotionally. Yet I will never forget the empathetic words he shared. "Now is the time for you to make new traditions with your kids. They don't have to look the same as they did before." His sincerity filled me with hope.

Knowing I was embracing his advice, I smiled as I glanced in the rearview mirror at my two boys. *It is time to create new memories together.* Empowered from my road trip earlier that year with Miss Jackie to my niece's wedding, I pulled out of the driveway and stepped on the gas, ready to begin our adventure.

The first leg of the trip was filled with laughter and fun times with college friends and their families who lived along the coast. Splashing in the ocean with other kids was a highlight for my boys. Deep, grown-up conversation fueled my soul and helped with the loneliness of making this trip without my husband.

We hugged, and I thanked my friends for their support as we prepared to leave for the second leg to explore Monterey and San Francisco, just the three of us. I am not sure if anyone saw the tears forming in the corner of my eyes. I was anxious about continuing on my own as the sole adult in a big city with my boys. I was worried about getting lost. Yet a small sliver of excitement about making memories together encouraged me to press on and brave the trail up the coast of California.

The next morning in Monterey, I woke up feeling lonesome. Not only was I missing the recent companionship of my friends, I could tell my kids were missing the fun adventures they'd had with their playmates. Realizing this was just the beginning of my new reality, I started to cry. *Why do I have to do life alone?* Feelings of uncertainty flooded my mind. *Can I even do this all by myself?*

Maybe you wish your circumstances were different too.

Perhaps you are single, and your heart's desire is to be married. You are in a season of delay.

It could be you desire to be a mom, but each month your pregnancy test is negative. You are in a season of pause.

Maybe you have a health issue or have suffered a job loss, and you are awaiting answers. You are in a season of uncertainty.

I don't know about you, but I do not like to wait. I search for the shortest line at the grocery store or guess which car will accelerate the fastest at a stoplight. I don't like to wait at a doctor's office or in line at Disneyland. FastPass was invented to help fellow impatient people like me. Don't even get me started about the DMV; that place about kills me.

When we are forced to stop and pause, our natural reaction is to cry out, *Why am I in this season of waiting?*

Let me introduce you to a man in the Bible who also had to wait. On fire for Christ, Paul was excited about his upcoming missionary journey to share the good news with others. However, his plans quickly changed when he found himself in prison instead.

To better understand a person in the Bible, I like to put myself in their shoes. What would I be thinking, feeling, or saying in their situation? Let's step into Paul's confusing predicament.

If I were Paul, I would cry out to God, pleading, "Lord, I don't understand why I am in jail. Don't you think my skills would be better utilized if I was out traveling the world and sharing Jesus with others? My ministry is winning others to Christ. Why did it come to a screeching halt? What good am I locked up in a cell all alone?"

Paul might not have been as dramatic, but I am sure he was puzzled about why he was sitting in a cell instead of out preaching. Perhaps you feel the same way. Your present situation just doesn't make sense.

You see only part of the picture, but God can see the bigger picture.

You observe only a piece of the puzzle, but God observes the entire completed puzzle.

You have only a finite view, but God has an infinite perspective.

God had an important purpose for Paul while he was incarcerated. During that time, he wrote letters to the churches he had visited on his earlier mission trips. Those letters became many of the New Testament books of the Bible: Romans, First and Second Corinthians, Galatians, Ephesians, Philippians, Colossians, First and Second Thessalonians, First and Second Timothy, Titus, and Philemon.

Paul's waiting period was the most significant part of his ministry.

Those letters have impacted millions of Christians and are still doing so today. From prison, Paul could not see the greater purpose God had planned for him.

Don't underestimate what God can do through *you* in your waiting time. Paul had more influence with his writing than he could ever have imagined. His impact after his death was greatly due to the letters he wrote in the very place he did not want to be.

Back in that hotel room in Monterey, I did not want to be there alone either. Going into the bathroom to cry, I opened my phone to a daily devotional to speak some truth into my heart. The entry for that morning reminded me God was with me and together we could confidently face life's challenges. The uplifting words also helped me realize that I had been asking the wrong question.

Instead of *Why am I alone*, God wanted to me to ask, *What do you want me to learn, Lord, as we walk through this together?*

God wants you to exchange your *why* with a *what*. Instead of questioning, *Why do you have me in this hard circumstance*, He wants you to ask, *What do you want to teach me as you guide me through this circumstance?*

Replace your uncertainty with trust and your narrow lens with God's wider scope. God has a bigger picture for your life than what you can see.

This new perspective does not come naturally to us. It involves daily surrendering our finite view and replacing it with God's infinite perspective. Then, instead of complaining about our circumstances, we can live in contentment knowing that God is working behind the scenes.

As Paul sat in jail, he modeled contentment for us.

> I am not saying this because I am in need, for I have learned to be content whatever the circumstances. I know what it is to be in need, and I know what it is to have plenty. I have learned the secret of being content in any and every situation, whether well fed or hungry, whether living in plenty or in want. I can do all this through him who gives me strength. (Philippians 4:11–13)

During our waiting periods, discontentment can emerge. I believe this is one of Satan's greatest tactics. He wants to distract us with things that could be, causing us to resent where we are. Discontentment makes us unable to be at peace with where God has us now. It blinds us from all the good, pulls us further from fulfilling the purpose God has for us, and steals our patience in His perfect timing.

Maybe Satan is using discontentment to sidetrack you from what God is trying to teach you in the waiting time. Listen to the secret to combat this: "I can do all things through Christ who gives me strength" (Philippians 4:13 BSB). Relying on God's powerful strength is the key to being content no matter the circumstances that you wish were different. All you need to do is ask Him for it.

Trusting God would give me the strength to continue our adventure. We traveled onward to San Francisco. We visited Alcatraz Island, rode bikes across the Golden Gate Bridge, and had huge ice cream sundaes at Ghirardelli's. It was my favorite part of my time with my boys, and never once during the trip did I feel alone again. Instead, I was seen, loved, and empowered by God's strength. As

I depended on Him to guide me, the vacation was life changing.

Don't underestimate what the Lord can do when you partner together with Him in your waiting season. Looking back, I can see that God was teaching me to trust Him even when I didn't have the full picture but only a tiny piece.

Where do you need to depend on God's strength and embrace the season He has you in? Where do you need to stop asking "why" and start asking something different? In Karen Ehman's book, *Let It Go*, she shares these great thought-provoking questions you can ask yourself:

- What does God want me to learn about Him that I might never discover if He were to suddenly pluck me out of this situation?
- What Christlike character traits is He trying to grow in me—patience, trust, compassion, faith?
- Who is watching—either up close or from afar—and discovering what God is like by my reactions to my current situation?
- How might my empathy for others deepen if I go through this current trial with grace and acceptance?
- What is God trying to say to me, not by the outcome, but through the voyage?[22]

God will use your answers to change your perspective. I know the waiting period is hard, and you wish your circumstances were different, but don't let Satan lure you into discontentment. Instead, hold on to the truth that you can do all things through Christ's strength. Ask for God to give patience as you wait on His perfect timing. Keep surrendering to God and find out what He wants you to discover during your times of uncertainty.

Your waiting period may be the most powerful place of growth in your life.

Like Paul in prison, your waiting period may be the most powerful place of growth in your life.

Let's Pray

God, thank You for partnering with me in my waiting season. If I am honest, I wish things were different. Help me see your perspective when all I can observe is a small sliver of the picture. I also ask today for Your strength to wait well. Remind me that I am not alone, and show me how to turn my *why* questions into *what* questions. I want my roots to grow deeper as I wait on Your perfect timing. In Jesus's name, Amen.

Truth

Replace your uncertainty with trust and your narrow lens with God's wider scope. God has a bigger picture for your life than what you can see.

Seek God and invite Him into your pain.

Tearfully allow yourself time to grieve and process the emotions.

Replace your finite view with God's infinite perspective.

Embrace God's character development in the midst of the chaos.

Never lose sight of God's grace.

Give praise to God even as your heart breaks.

Trust God is good when your mind is doubting and you don't understand.

Honestly share your story and help another hurting heart.

11

Growing Deeper Roots

But blessed are those who trust in the Lord
and have made the Lord their hope and confidence.
They are like trees planted along a riverbank,
with roots that reach deep into the water.
Such trees are not bothered by the heat
or worried by long months of drought.
Their leaves stay green, and
they never stop producing fruit.
Jeremiah 17:7–8 NLT

Another Saturday morning in my backyard with a piece of pottery.

However, this time, I was not intending to break it. This giant pot was a gift.

When I drove home from the hospital after my surgery with Dr. Linzey, I found the huge, beautiful pot and fruit tree on my doorstep. In lieu of flowers, our friends had given us a tree to plant in memory of our baby. *What a brilliant idea,* I thought. *Flowers will eventually die, but we can have this fruit tree forever.*

The day had come to plant their thoughtful gift.

My husband and Kyle rolled the huge container to the center of our yard. Jumping up and down, my three-year-old was thrilled to help—but his excitement was a stark contrast to my sadness and sorrow.

Planting the tree was going to be more emotional than I had anticipated.

As we poured the potting soil, the fresh dirt was warm to my hands—my empty hands. I started crying. *I should be holding my sweet baby in my arms, not planting a tree in her memory.* Another wave of grief hit me. My heart felt like it was breaking all over again.

The loss was real. Tears continued to roll down my face as we physically rooted the tree into the large ceramic container. My friends had thought of everything by providing the pot. In case we ever moved, we could take our special remembrance tree with us.

I don't want to forget my precious baby. I snapped another photo.

Trying to capture this unforgettable event, I later framed a priceless photo of all three of us smiling and crouched down next to the beautiful memory tree. I have one hand on the edge of the pot and my other arm embracing my family. For the longest time, I could not keep myself from stopping at the mantle and staring at that picture.

Little did I know how God was going to use trees to teach me so much about growing deeper in my faith.

Fast-forward ten years later. I was inside a bookstore, and once again I found myself enthralled with another image of a tree. It was strikingly green and extremely healthy on the outside, but what caught my eye was what was underneath. Almost as large as the branches above, the tree had an intricate and deep root system below it.

This tree was pictured on the cover of the book, *Thrive*, written by Mark Hall, the lead singer of Casting Crowns. In his book, he shares about a large oak tree in South Alabama. More than 300 years old, it is strong and sturdy and located where two rivers come together. A farmer once told him, "You know, the reason these kinds of trees are so strong is, not only are they planted by the water, but they have just as much going on under the ground as they do above the ground."[23]

I don't know if you have ever really thought about what is happening underground. Since our eyes cannot see roots, our minds may think they are unimportant to the overall health of the tree. Nothing can be further from the truth. For a tree to remain strong, it needs a root system that expands just as wide beneath the soil as its branches reach above ground.

Stop and visualize this with me. Think about the massive branches of a tree. They extend high, fanning out to reach for the sunlight. They stretch in all directions allowing for new leaves to develop. Now picture this same vast growth under the tree, below the dirt where no one can see it. Imagine how the roots spread out wide and plunge down deep to match the substantial expansion of the tree above.

That tree has depth.

Depth. God had planted this word in my mind just months earlier while I was sitting in an airplane coming home from vacation with my boys. I did not realize how much that word was going to change my life.

As I stood in that bookstore staring at the photograph of the book cover, I thought, *What if God wants me to grow my roots deeper in my faith just like this tree?*

Deep roots are essential for trees to be able to endure strong winds and floods. Without depth, gusts of wind and raging water can easily knock over a tree.

Just as a tree needs depth to withstand the storms of life, God wants us to grow deep roots in our faith to endure difficulties in our lives.

Trees are a powerful reminder to get rooted. As Jeremiah 17:7–9 illustrates, those who trust in the Lord and have placed their hope and confidence in Him are like deeply rooted trees that stay green and fruitful and are not bothered by the heat and drought. They thrive even in the harshest conditions.

Are you rooted? If a storm came blowing into your life right now, have you grown deep enough roots in your faith to handle it?

My prayer is that we can dig deeper into God's Word every day to grow a massive root system. Then we will not be troubled by the

Could it be that God wants to grow us deeper, so He can take us higher than we ever knew possible?

unexpected, but will continue to be healthy and bear fruit, just like Jeremiah teaches us.

But what if deep roots are not just to help us survive? What if they enable us to grow and thrive? Could it be that God wants to grow us deeper so He can take us higher than we ever knew possible?

Let me paraphrase a story from Tony Evans's book, *Detours*.

> A man walked into the woods to have one last conversation with God. He was disappointed with his life and ready to quit. "I don't know why You have me stuck in this same situation with no change," he cried out to the Lord. "Give me one good reason why I should not give up."
>
> God immediately replied, "Look around. What do you see?"
>
> Surprised by the question, the man replied, "I see both ferns and bamboo."
>
> "Yes," God said, "both fern and bamboo seeds were planted. I gave them proper sunlight, watered them daily, and took good care of both. Immediately, the ferns started growing. Quickly, they became green and lush. However, the bamboo did not grow at all the first year."
>
> The Lord continued, "The second year, the ferns became even more abundant and vibrant. However, there was still no growth from the bamboo. The same thing happened the third and fourth years. Finally, in the fifth year, a tiny sprout appeared, and a small shoot of bamboo began to emerge from the earth."
>
> God then asked the man, "How tall is the bamboo in front of you?"
>
> The man answered, "It's over one hundred feet tall."
>
> "You are right," the Lord said. "In order for bamboo to sustain that height, it needed to grow strong, deep roots under the surface for the first five years of

its life. From the outside, it looked like I had given up on the bamboo because there was no external growth taking place. But I was working on the most import- ant part, the inner growth." Then God added, "You see, I knew the bamboo would eventually grow to over one hundred feet tall, so I knew it needed to be deeply grounded first. The same is true for you."

New hope was unleashed in the man's heart. "The in- side growth that no one else sees allows Me to take you to the height I had planned for you all along." God said. "I have not given up on you. I am still writing your story."[24]

Friend, God is not finished with your story either.

I love what Tony Evans says about this parable of the fern and the bamboo. He teaches, "If God is taking a long time with you on your detour, it is because He is trying to take you deeper on the inside first. He is trying to develop and strengthen you to sustain the destiny in store. His plan for you is high. His calling for you is tall. His purpose for you will one day soar. But just as you can't build a skyscraper on a chicken-coop foundation, you can't place a divine destiny on a shallow soul. The higher your mountains, the deeper your valleys will seem. And difficult roads often lead to the most magnificent destinations."[25]

Your struggles and challenges are deepening your faith. They are developing strong roots in you so God can take you higher than you ever imagined. He wants you and me to soar. I don't know about you, but this gives me amazing hope.

When I see the word *soar*, it makes me think of an eagle flying high above the clouds. Did you know that eagles are the only birds who fly higher in a storm? Other birds will find shelter, but not the eagle. They allow the strong winds of the raging storm to lift them skyward, propelling them to new altitudes.

Do you want to rise to greater heights in the middle of the hard times in your life? Soaring has little to do with our strength and everything to do with depending on God's strength. Therefore, it is not about striving for more, but surrendering to God's plan. Yet God will only take us higher after He has grown us deeper.

"Those who hope in the Lord will renew their strength. They will soar on wings like eagles" (Isaiah 40:31). If you want to rise above your storm, it is essential to put your hope in God and fully trust that He has a greater plan beyond your wildest imagination. Remember, the higher He wants you to soar, the deeper you first need to go in your relationship with Him.

In the middle of the waiting, when God is working on your internal, unseen growth, I encourage you to ponder and answer these questions for yourself.

- What change is God asking me to make on the inside so I can be taken higher on the outside?

- What perspective shift do I need to make regarding my present circumstances?

- What action step can I take today to grow my roots deeper so I can rise to greater heights in the future?

As I reflect back on the day I planted the special remembrance tree, I had no clue the plans God had for me. I had no idea that He would birth a ministry out of my pain and start a podcast, *Depth*, to encourage others to grow deeper in their faith.

That day, all I could see was heartbreak. I could not see the beginning of the internal growth. Like the bamboo, it would be years before I would see any external growth. But God was still working.

Don't give up. Allow God to refine you into the person He made you to be. Focus on the truth that He is developing your character and preparing you for His purpose. Embrace the process of growing deeper roots so that if God wants to make you 100-foot-tall bamboo, you are ready!

Let's Pray

> *God*, thank You for using trees to show me the impor-
> tance of depth. I want to grow deep roots as I trust Your
> plans for my life. I know it is not always easy, so fill me
> with Your strength each day. Like the verse in Isaiah, I
> want to soar like the eagle above my unexpected storm.
> Show me areas in my life that need deeper growth and
> help me embrace the character development. In Jesus's
> name, Amen.

Truth

> Develop deep roots so God can take you to new heights.

12

Embrace the Chisel

I will put into the fire; I will refine them
like silver and test them like gold.
They will call on my name
and I will answer them; I will say,
"They are my people," and they will say,
"The LORD is our God."
Zechariah 13:9

It was difficult to hear the truth.

"I want to walk away from this better, not bitter," I said to Anita over the loud noise at a crowded restaurant. Sitting in a corner booth, she listened as I shared what God was teaching me in counseling as I processed the hurt and pain from my divorce.

She understood that all too well; my friend had walked through the same storm just a couple of years earlier. I cherished our time together. She completely related to everything I was feeling and experiencing. That was why her words, hard as they were to hear, had such power.

"Jodi, you are getting stuck here. I think you know what you need to do."

Stunned, I did not want to admit she was correct.

As I considered how to move forward, my mind flashed back to the summer of 2011 when I read the transformative book, *How We Love Our Kids,* by Milan and Kay Yerkovich.[26] This book opened my eyes to see how inconsistencies in my childhood emotional security were affecting my parenting and marriage. The chapter on the vacillator had perfectly described me. Every word. Every emotion. Vacillating between the strong connection times with my loved ones to quickly seeing only the negative when hard times arose, I struggled to navigate those two extremes.

Learning how to deal with my negative emotions had become my life mission after reading that section. I wanted to understand more.

Self-awareness is the key to change. Little did I know how much this statement would impact my life.

The following summer in 2012, I read another life-changing book to better understand myself on this road of self-discovery. In *Unglued* by Lysa TerKeurst[27], I identified myself as an exploder, a person who outwardly overreacts to others. I asked myself the questions, *Why am I so prone to blow up at my loved ones? What is triggering this anger, and why do I blame everyone else around me?* The book challenged me to look at my feelings as indicators of something that needed to be addressed instead of giving in to my emotions.

From then on, my self-awareness was on high alert. I dug deeper into my past to reveal things that I never knew before. Through counseling, I learned that anger is a secondary emotion while hurt, disappointment, fear, or worry are primary emotions. As a result, I began dealing with primary emotions instead of just erupting with anger.

That growth step of learning to identify the real trigger behind my anger took time. True change never happens immediately. Growth is slow and does not occur overnight. As I became more aware, I realized that how I reacted to my emotions had caused my family deep pain. That greatly saddened me.

When we met that night in the restaurant, Anita was fully aware of my self-awareness journey—which gave her the wisdom to speak the truth to me in love. "Jodi, I know you have been working hard on breaking this negative pattern in your life, but I can see you are still stuck every time you talk about why your marriage fell apart."

She was right. I would only focus on him, even though it was clear I had contributed to our marriage problems. Each of us had brought our own hurts and struggles to the relationship. My reactivity had caused him lots of pain, resulting in him pulling away.

Before our dinner entrées arrived, Anita graciously said, "I think you need to share this with him, maybe write him a letter."

Deep down, I knew there was truth in her words, but everything in me fought back against that advice. *Could God be asking me to humble myself and be vulnerable to the very person who broke my heart?*

At that moment, the seed was planted, and God started to water it that weekend while my kids were away visiting their dad. Instead of displacing the blame, I decided it was time for me to own my part. Honestly, I had admitted it to my counselor, my close friends, and even myself, but I had never shared it with him.

I realize now that God was refining me through this healing process, even though I did not enjoy it. No one likes to be put in the refiner's fire.

A silversmith uses the fire to purify precious metal. Placing the silver over the flame, the intense heat burns away any impurities. To ensure that the metal is not destroyed, he intently watches it through the whole refining process. The silver is fully refined when the silversmith can see his image in it.

God refines us the same way.

Just as silver is put in the fire to remove the impurities, God uses our struggles to clear away our impurities.

Just as the silver reflects the image of the silversmith when it is fully refined, we will reflect the image of God.

The goal of the refinement process is to make us more like Christ.

Chiseling away at my pride, God was growing me. Stripping away my bitterness, God was stretching me. The whole process was difficult but necessary.

With God's help, I wrote that letter, taking full ownership of my part in the failure of the marriage. I shared how I wished I had become self-aware sooner. I wrote how I regretted the hurtful words spoken to him that did not help us grow closer, and I apologized for blaming him. It was not easy to admit any of it, but those words helped me break free and become unstuck. They were a big step on my road to healing.

God may not be asking you to write a letter, but He does want you to become more self-aware. Maybe He is inviting you to dive deeper into your past so you can identify your triggers. Perhaps God knows you need to gain new perspective to better understand yourself.

God is refining you, developing your character so you can become the best version of you. I know growth and change are not easy, but let's embrace the chisel.

Lysa TerKeurst's book *Forgiving What You Can't Forget* is full of helpful self-awareness tips. In "Collecting the Dots," "Connecting the Dots," and "Correcting the Dots," my three favorite chapters, Lysa encourages us to "make connections between what happened to us in our growing up years with the reasons we do some of the things we do, say some of the things we say, and believe some of the things we believe right now."[28]

So much of who we are today stems from our childhood. Have you ever thought back to your younger years and tried to remember struggles you had growing up? Making an inventory of the pain and hurt you experienced as a child or teenager will help you make connections to triggers you experience in the present.

As I dove deeper into my childhood and tried to understand why I identified with the vacillator and exploder, I was collecting the dots. During that time, I remember praying daily for God to bring important memories to my mind; I even asked my siblings about what they remembered. Sometimes it is hard to recall your childhood, so putting your memories down on paper is a great way to begin.

Lysa adds, "Those things that happen in our lives don't just tell a story. They inform us of the story we tell ourselves. If we listen carefully, woven throughout our narratives is a belief system that formed inside of us as children."[29]

After looking into our past, we then need to make connections to our reactions. Meeting with a counselor weekly was pivotal in helping me connect the dots. Maybe you are wondering why you are triggered so easily. My counselor told me, "If it is hysterical, it is historical." Our overreactions usually connect to something painful in our childhood.

Here is one exercise I learned from my therapist. Since anger is a secondary emotion, each time you feel it erupting inside, try to pause and record what happened just before you were triggered. Did someone disappoint you or say hurtful words to you? Perhaps your circumstances stirred up fear and worry. Identify the emotion behind the anger and see if there a pattern each time. As you trace these negative emotions and what circumstances activated them, you will begin to connect them to the past and identify your triggers.

Maybe you don't struggle with anger like I do but tend to withdraw. Ask yourself what happened that caused you to want to retreat. Put words to the emotions that you are feeling and see if there is a connection to anything in your past. This self-awareness will be vital as you try to correct the dots.

In counseling, these were called growth steps, new ways to look at negative emotions and react to them. With this new awareness, we hopefully do not fall back into old thought patterns and reactions as quickly. Instead, we look at life through a new lens. For

Your response is your responsibility.

me, writing the letter was my way of correcting the dots.

One of my favorite sayings that I learned through those tough years was "My response is my responsibility." I cannot control how someone treats me or what they say to me, but I can control how I react to them with the words I choose to speak and the tone I use to say them.

Your response is your responsibility. I encourage you to make a list of your own growth steps, addressing the areas where you want to grow and change. As you do, you will start to correct the dots.

As you become more self-aware and see connections from your past to your present, I pray you see self-awareness as a gift that God is using to refine you.

Lysa writes, "If we become more self-aware of how we are processing our thoughts and perceptions and redirect those in more life-giving ways then inside every loss, a more wise, empathetic, understanding, discerning, compassionate person of strength and humility has the potential to rise with us."[30]

Friend, this is what I want for you. I want you to become more wise, empathetic, and compassionate. I want you to be able to discern and understand more about yourself and why you respond the way you do.

All of this requires hard work, but I believe it is so worth it. Owning your choices and admitting mistakes does not come naturally. Don't get discouraged when old patterns rise up in you. Take responsibility, repair the brokenness between you and your family, and keep growing more and more like Your Maker each day.

Let's Pray

God, open my eyes to see self-awareness as a gift. I pray I can embrace the refining process as You chisel and mold me into the person You created me to be! I know it is not easy, and growth takes time, so fill me with Your strength. Help me dig deeper and see connections from my past to my present. Empower me to take growth steps to change. I genuinely want to reflect the image of Christ to my loved ones. In Jesus's name, Amen.

Truth

Self-awareness is a gift and the key to change. Change takes intentionality.

13

The Bless in the Mess

Look carefully then how you walk,
not as unwise but as wise,
making the best use of the time,
because the days are evil.
Ephesians 5:15–16 ESV

It was truly such a gift.

All my burdens started to float away as I opened my car door and immediately felt the ocean breeze against my face. The smell of the coastal air and the soothing sound of the crashing waves calmed my troubled soul.

I smiled as I thought, *The beach is my happy place!*

Walking barefoot through the sand, the soft heat of the sun also brought warmth to my anxious heart. Staring out over the beautiful ocean view in front of me, I knew this was just want I needed to rejuvenate.

The past two months had been a whirlwind. The aftershock of Jeannie's cancer news had caused a cyclone of stress and negative emotion. Additional doctor appointments. Chemotherapy sessions every other week. Carpool schedules for Jeannie's kids as she was too ill to drive them. It was like a hurricane had blown in, and we were all still reeling from its effects.

As Jeannie focused on her treatment, all of her friends and I offered to carry the extra load. From delivering meals to organizing drop-offs and pickups for her children and driving Jeannie to and from chemotherapy appointments, we all jumped in to help.

One Friday afternoon, my phone rang. As I answered, I could hear the distress in Jeannie's faint voice. *Something is wrong.* I asked her, "Are you okay?"

She told me she was having severe pain in her abdomen and needed to see the doctor before the office closed for the weekend. Her husband was still not home from work, so she asked if I could drive her.

"I will be there in ten minutes," I said, knowing it must be urgent. I dropped off my kids with a friend and bolted to her house.

On that drive, Jeannie and I cried lots of tears. Some were over the agony and discomfort she was experiencing and others about the stress on her family, but most of the sobbing happened when we talked about her prognosis. The oncologist had been honest and upfront with Jeannie, revealing that the chemo would not stop the stage 4 cancer, but it might buy her some time. We hoped it could give her extra months or even years to spend with her husband and children.

With that looming diagnosis, time suddenly looked very different for my dear friend. It was no longer a luxury. It seemed more like a stopwatch counting backward. Each minute with her family became a precious gift.

Sitting in my beach chair looking at the ocean, I had a similar revelation after walking through my divorce.

Time was important before our family split, but I honestly never saw it as priceless. Now that I had to share my days with my kids, time looked completely different to me too. It was now a treasure, and every second I had with my children held much value, like an expensive jewel that needed to be protected. I began guarding the hours with my boys as well as the ones without.

The minutes with my kids became precious and purposeful.

The minutes without my kids became deliberate and intentional.

Embracing this new insight, I carried my chair to an empty spot along the beach. Sitting there alone, I realized that I had the entire stretch of coastline to myself. It was just God and me. Pulling out my Bible and journal, I started to ponder everything from the past months.

Writing about my feelings was therapeutic. I was overwhelmed and depleted from carrying the weight of two families. Physically worn out from the extra hours helping my friend, I honestly shared my struggle with managing it all as a single mom. Add on the emotional exhaustion from watching Jeannie fight for her life, and it is no wonder I wrote, "Most days, it is more than I can handle."

That day on the beach, I was thankful for the gift of time to rest, reflect, and reboot.

Each of us is given exactly the same amount of time. We have twenty-four hours in a day. We have seven days in a week. This equals 168 hours per week. How we use this limited resource is up to us.

Instead of letting it slip away, I started to deliberately plan and "unplan" our schedules. I wanted to slow down and truly enjoy the minutes I did have with my boys. I called those special instances joy moments. It could be a simple word spoken, a hug, or an actual activity or event. In the middle of the hard times, I appreciated how amazing these joy moments truly were.

I also realized how precious my time with Jeannie was. Driving her back and forth to her appointments became an occasion to go deep and talk about what really mattered. We reminisced about being a mom in the early years. When the kids were newborn babies, the minutes just seemed to creep forward. Middle-of-the-night feedings and the multiple diaper changes in a day made the hours go by so slowly. Years with toddlers and preschoolers seemed to have the same effect. The hours to naptime dawdled and drifted and those long afternoons until bedtime seemed to last forever.

It was good for our souls to look back. Jeannie and I smiled in the car as we recalled a phone conversation the morning after both Conor and Lucas did not sleep a wink as babies. Both feeling like a truck had hit us, we had no idea how we were going to parent our firstborns. There were many days when we felt like that. Overwhelmed. Exhausted.

As we reminisced, one question kept circling in my head. *Did I make the most of every opportunity with my kids?* I remember my boys asking for me to play Legos or build blocks with them on the floor. I would be there physically, but my mind was often preoccupied with emails or to-do lists. I so wished I could go back and be fully present with them.

Being intentional means you make the most of every minute, every day, and every week.

What if I told you that you have only 936 weeks from when you bring home your newborn baby until they are eighteen years old? Just a little less than 1,000 weeks under your roof where you can intentionally speak truth to them, build their character, and teach your kids about faith.

A couple of years ago at church, a guest pastor spoke on this idea. With a large glass container filled to the top with 1,000 marbles, he dramatically showed us visually just how many weeks we had with our children. Dumping out almost the entire jar, there were only 200 marbles remaining. I gasped as he said, "This is the amount of time you have left if you have a high school freshman." Honestly, it was shocking to see the small amount sitting in the jar. That year, my son had just completed his freshman year, so I realized that our weeks together were even less.

Are you being intentional with each marble? Are you guarding your time with your kids to make the most of each week? All of us have the same quantity of minutes, but the quality of our time is completely up to us. Making a list

> **All of us have the same quantity of minutes, but the quality of our time is completely up to us.**

of the top priorities I wanted to implement, I proceeded to carve out space on my calendar to make them happen.

Time with my kids

- Family meals: eat together and talk about our day around the dinner table.
- Grow in our faith: as a family, go to church, pray, and read devotionals together.
- Fun nights: game nights, movie nights, and lots of laughter.
- Learn together: read books and do schoolwork.
- Make special memories: family vacations and weekend trips.
- Enjoy the outdoors: hikes, bike rides, and adventures.

Time without my kids

- Daily: spend alone time with God.
- Depth: read and grow.
- Rest: recharge and reboot.
- Community: connect with friends.

My day at the beach was an example of that kind of intentional living. Instead of seeing my day without my kids as negative, I saw it as a gift to recharge and grow—the "bless in the mess!"

Do you have your own bless in the mess? Maybe your job loss is allowing you more intentional hours with your family. Perhaps the cancer diagnosis has ignited a spark in you to be fully present in every moment with your family. Maybe the divorce has opened your eyes to see time as a gift.

I believe our difficult circumstances can be the very catalyst to our growth. Hard times are fertile times for God to open our eyes to places we need to grow. It is not always fun in the middle of those tough conditions, but the character development is always worth it.

Where is God asking you to grow? Spiritually, does God want you to dive deeper in His Word and grow your roots? Maybe He is asking you to exercise your faith muscles and grow your trust and dependence on Him. Emotionally, is God asking you to work on your reactivity? Relationally, is God asking you to have more patience?

God does not want us to stay spiritual and emotional babies, so He uses one of His biggest growing tools—pain. C. S. Lewis wrote, "God whispers to us in our pleasures, speaks in our consciences, but shouts in our pains. It is his megaphone to rouse a deaf world."[31]

This gives me a new perspective on my heartbreak. God is taking my hurt and growing me into the person He wants me to be. He is using your hard situations to grow your character too.

He is using your pain to open your eyes to places that have become stagnant. He is developing your mind and changing your heart as you depend on Him for strength. God is working and helping you grow into the best version of you.

Today, I encourage you to find your bless in the mess. Is God helping you react more lovingly? Is He working on your mind so you can take each thought captive? Is He asking you to be more purposeful with your days?

For me, my bless in the mess was seeing time as a gift and living with intention.

At the beach, I had been gifted with a few hours to work on me. I knew I needed to recharge so I could be the best mom I could be for my boys as well as reboot so I could pour out to my friend and her family. No longer wasting any minutes, I deliberately chose to spend my day with God. Reading, growing, and learning with the sound of crashing waves and the ocean breeze against my face was the best choice for me.

Let me encourage you to not waste your minutes, hours, or weeks. I know the days seem long, but the years are short and fly by quickly.

Truly enjoy your time with your little ones as you cuddle your babies. When your preschooler is building blocks, kneel down on the carpet with them and fully engage and play with them. I know laundry needs to get done, but you will never get that hour back if you miss it. When your young elementary-aged student needs help writing his letters or reading a book, connect with him. When your junior high student needs to share about her day, be fully present and listen to her. Don't let your mind wander to grocery lists or dinner prep. Before you know it, your child will be in high school with less than 200 weeks left with you.

Remember, we are not all guaranteed these years with our loved ones. Just like Jeannie discovered, time is a precious gift. Let's live with intention.

Let's Pray

> *God,* thank You for opening my eyes to see time as a gift. I pray I can create joy moments with my loved ones and live with purpose. Help me continue to see each marble in the jar as precious. Allow me to see the bless in the mess and trust Your plan even when I don't understand. I want You to grow my roots deeper in my faith than ever before. In Jesus's name, Amen."

Truth

> Guard your time and be intentional.

<u>S</u>eek God and invite Him into your pain.

<u>T</u>earfully allow yourself time to grieve and process the emotions.

<u>R</u>eplace your finite view with God's infinite perspective.

<u>E</u>mbrace God's character development in the midst of the chaos.

<u>N</u>ever lose sight of God's grace.

<u>G</u>ive praise to God even as your heart breaks.

<u>T</u>rust God is good when your mind is doubting and you don't understand.

<u>H</u>onestly share your story and help another hurting heart.

14

A Divine Appointment

For I am convinced that neither death nor life,
neither angels nor demons,
neither the present nor the future,
nor any powers, neither height
nor depth, nor anything else in all creation,
will be able to separate us from the love of God
that is in Christ Jesus our Lord.
Romans 8:38–39

I had no idea what God had planned for me.

"Your ticket please," the attendant at the door asked in a kind voice. I handed it to her and followed a line of people into the large, crowded arena. Thousands of ladies shuffled to their seats ready to be encouraged at the Christian women's conference, and their loud, enthusiastic chatter echoed through the stadium seating. Excited to finally catch my breath after the long week, I plopped down in my chair.

This weekend away is just want I needed. Emotionally exhausted, physically fatigued, and spiritually drained, life as a single mom was taking its toll on me.

As the worship band started to play, a large weight lifted off me. The music touched my heart, and the song lyrics fueled my soul. Feeling God's presence with each note, I was hopeful that this weekend convention of Christian women would not only recharge me, but change my perspective as well.

For the past nine months, I had been working weekly with my counselor on all the negative feelings I was experiencing. We discussed sadness and anger, but there was one emotion I still needed to address. Honestly, I didn't fully understand how firmly it was sitting in the dark recesses of my mind, influencing my thoughts. Deep inside, I felt like I was a failure because my marriage had failed. Shame was rendering me useless, and I was not sure how to overcome it.

I believed I had disappointed God so much that my ministry to serve Him was forever tainted. The same disgraceful message kept repeating in my head: *God can no longer use me because I am divorced.*

Perhaps you are feeling deep shame over a past choice or your present situation. I want you to know that God does not want you to stay stuck there. He does not want you to be shackled in shame. Instead, He desires for you to live in freedom by His grace.

Grace. I had learned all about that word growing up. By God's grace, I had been saved through faith. I understood it for my salvation, but I could not see how it applied to my current situation.

As a perfectionist, I was tough on myself. I could not let myself off the hook. I remained chained to the negative chatter in my head.

God knew I needed to hear the truth, so He gave me a divine appointment, a moment in time when He places someone in our path for a specific reason. A divine appointment is a special way God speaks to us. I do not believe in coincidences. I trust in God's providence. He is purposeful.

I believe God delights in setting up these special meetings when we are in the middle of grief. He wants to show us that He cares, and He will use close friends, family, and sometimes people we have never met to speak His truth to us and give us hope.

My divine appointment came as I listened to Lisa Bevere speak at the women's conference. Ironically, I had never heard of Lisa before that weekend. I had actually come to see my favorite author, Lysa TerKeurst, talk about her new book.

But God had other plans in store for me when Lisa Bevere took the stage. Her passion captivated the entire audience, and her bold words about spiritual warfare from her book, *Girls With Swords*, pierced my heart. She powerfully preached. "I believe the attacks on your life have much more to do with who you might be in the future than who you have been in the past."[32]

Sitting up in my chair, I felt like those words were directed right at me. I leaned in to hear more.

Lisa continued with a story of how she learned that profound truth while watching the movie *Terminator* with her son. In the 1984 film, a woman named Sarah Connor faces an assassin from the future known as the Terminator (played by Arnold Schwarzenegger), who has transported in time to try to kill her. A defender also arrives to protect her, revealing that Sarah will be a hero and a legend in later years.

Super confused about why she is a target, she says to her protector, "I didn't do anything." He responds, "But you will."[33]

Right then, Lisa had realized that our enemy often knows who we are in Christ before we do.

She spoke boldly into the microphone. "Satan has made it his aim to distract us from becoming who we really are meant to be and to stop us from living out the purpose God has given us."

Then she repeated those powerful words, "I believe the attacks on your life have much more to do with who you might be in the future than who you have been in the past."

That truth changed my life.

Up until then, I felt like I was a failure because my marriage had failed. I believed Satan had won and God could not use me. But Lisa's message made me look deeper.

What if Satan knew that God had big plans for me when I didn't? What if the spiritual attacks on me were not about who I was but about who I was going to become? This sparked immense hope within my spirit.

After hearing Lisa's message, I realized that Satan wanted me to stay stuck in a place of shame. He loved that I felt like a failure. He enjoyed how my pain and brokenness made me feel useless in God's eyes.

Through it all, he was distracting me from God's plan.

What if Satan is distracting you from God's plan too? The enemy wants you to think you are a disappointment and the Lord cannot use you. He does not want you to know that God could use your pain and your brokenness to help others.

I have news for you. God is the God of Grace. He has already died on the cross for your sins, and He can restore anything you place at the foot of His cross. A divorce. An addiction. A choice from your past. Whatever is making you feel deep shame.

Satan does not want you to become the person God created you to be, so he piles on the guilt—but don't let him win. Just like Lisa showed me at the conference, the spiritual attacks are not about who you were then, but about who you are going to become.

It is crazy to me now to think how Satan's deceptive plan had almost worked on me. But God knew that I would be sitting in that audience, and He knew that Lisa's words would touch my heart in such a deep way that I would never be the same again. I am so thankful for His divine appointment.

From that weekend onward, I was determined to become this woman that God already knew I could be. I was not going to let Satan get the last word. I was on fire, and nothing could stop me.

I remember saying to Satan, "You almost had me. I had truly felt broken and useless. But now I am on to you and your tactics."

I began saying, and then shouting this phrase over and over. "I may have a broken heart, but I am not a broken vessel. God can still use me!"

That was a pivotal change in my journey with the Lord. Before it, I knew God was walking with me and helping me through my grief and pain, but I still believed I had let Him down. I felt "less than," like my brokenness had disqualified me.

Maybe you feel like your brokenness has disqualified you. I want to encourage you today with this truth: your brokenness qualifies you even more. Your broken story is the very ingredient God can use to help another heart.

> **Your broken story is the very ingredient God can use to help another heart.**

First, God wants to use your pain to help you grow your character and to chisel you more and more into His masterpiece. Do you want to become the best version of you?

Second, God is in the business of redeeming your pain for His plans. This usually involves sharing your hurt with others, comforting them through circumstances similar to the ones you lived out months or years earlier, and being vulnerable enough to say the words *me too* and *I know exactly how you are feeling*. This positions you to encourage and support them through their heartbreak and pain.

Who better to help someone through an addiction than someone who has experienced freedom from addiction?

Who better to comfort someone grieving the loss of a loved one than someone who has experienced comfort during their loss?

Who better to offer hope to someone who is walking through a divorce than someone who has walked that same path?

Who better to comfort someone struggling with infertility than someone who also struggled with getting pregnant?

Who better to support someone who has just received the diagnosis of cancer than someone who has walked the same path of chemotherapy?

God wants to use you. Your heartbreak can be redeemed, no matter the cause. Satan does not get the last word. With the Lord's strength, you can terminate his lies with the truth.

I have discovered that God has an amazing purpose for each one of us! To remind myself of this, I placed a sign in my bathroom that I read every morning right before I take my shower. "Be the kind of woman that when your feet hit the floor each morning, the devil says, 'Oh crap, she's up.'"

Remember, you have a choice whether to live shackled in shame or free in grace. Don't let Satan's lies render you useless. Instead, make him regret ever trying to derail you from your purpose. Together, let's shout out to the devil, *You have messed with the wrong person. Go back to hell where you belong because I choose to live free by God's amazing grace!*

Every day, make an intentional choice to walk the path of freedom, knowing God can use your brokenness to His glory!

Let's Pray

> *God*, thank You for speaking truth to me through Your divine appointments in my life. I pray Lisa's words will resonate deep in my heart. Help me break free from the shackles of shame and live by grace. Allow me to recognize Satan's tactics and stop him from distracting me from the purpose You created for me. God, I want You to use my story to help others and to grow my roots deeper in You. In Jesus's name, Amen.

Truth

> Live free with grace, not shackled with shame.

15

Be Vulnerable

Being confident of this,
that he who began a good work in you
will carry it on to completion
until the day of Christ Jesus.
Philippians 1:6

I wished I could keep it a secret.

Sitting on the couch in my therapist's office, I felt safe to share. That was good because I had so much, almost too much, to share. It felt like more than one person could handle.

What will people think? What if others find out? These thoughts had circled daily, sometimes hourly in my mind. Embarrassed, I kept wondering how others would react once they knew my family was going through a divorce.

My close friends were aware, but that was all. The kids were not ready to tell their friends, so we kept it private as we grieved. But the news was going to get out soon. That was the reality.

Neighbors knew that I had faith in God. Others in the community saw that my family attended Saddleback Church, and we had even led small groups in our home. People understood that we were strong Christians.

Will they judge me? Will they gossip about me when I am not around?

Shame was my new middle name. I wore it in secret, scared of how others would critique me.

As I confided this fear to my therapist, she listened to me share my distress about disappointing others. Honestly, I did not want them to look down on me. An amazing counselor, she helped me to ask myself a deeper question.

Why was I so worried what others thought?

I had just returned from the women's retreat empowered by Lisa's words and excited about God's plan for my life. But I was still living in fear of what others would say when they found out my family was breaking apart. Even though I had made big progress at the conference, Satan still had a grip on me. I wanted to be free of it.

God had already been working on me, preparing me how to overcome this fear. Some of my best quality time with the Lord was in the early morning hours when my kids were still sleeping. It was not uncommon for me to be up at 4:00 or 5:00 a.m. either reading or journaling.

One morning, just a couple of days after my insightful conversation with my counselor, I felt God asking me to sit at my computer and type instead of writing in my journal. As I started to tap the keys, something exciting started to happen. It was one of those moments where I felt God speaking through me, and I just wrote what I felt Him saying.

He was asking me to be completely vulnerable—and it was totally freeing! I couldn't pound out the words fast enough!

Then I felt God asking me to send what I had just written to everyone in my inbox.

My heart started to beat faster. *There is no way I can do that!*

But as I again read what I wrote, I felt God was asking me to step out of my comfort zone and fully trust Him.

So, I did it. Here is that email. I titled it "Vulnerability."

I have heard the word vulnerable multiple times in the last day. To me, this word means being completely authentic and open, sharing the real you! However, being vulnerable can have two results: you can receive judgment from others when you show the real you, or the real you can offer encouragement to others. Sadly, both results happen when you are vulnerable; one of the risks to being vulnerable. In this day and age, with Facebook and social media, we only see the good times in people's lives, however, not many people share what happens behind the closed doors of their home. What if more people shared their behind-the-scenes footage? What if more people were vulnerable, showing the authentic side of them: the good, the bad, and the ugly?

So, here is me being completely vulnerable–I hope this brings you encouragement and not judgment.

2014 has been the hardest year of my life. At the end of January, I received heartbreaking news that crushed me. My marriage of 15 1/2 years was ending. Honestly, I will never forget that day! For months, I was in deep grief; I had all the emotions: shock, anger, sadness . . . Lots of tears and lots of journaling! Friend, I am here to say that God is faithful in the hard times, more than you can ever understand. There is a verse in Psalms that says that God is close to the brokenhearted, and I am living proof of that. You are never alone! God is always there with you! This last year, I have experienced God in a way that I have never experienced before. I have learned that God cares about you so much, even the littlest details that we sometimes think don't matter. God wants to use us, even in our brokenness! One common theme that I am learning is that God uses our pain; I am not sure why we have to go through some of these hard times that we do encounter, but I am confident to say that he never wastes that hurt. You may have a broken heart, but you are not a broken vessel. Honestly, I say this to myself all the time; I may have a broken heart, but I am not a broken vessel. God, please still use me.

Friend, no matter what you have experienced. It could be going through a divorce like me, or it could be losing a loved one or another hard time. God can use that pain! He wants to take you from a place of heartbreak to a place of strength. You can only get there by completely relying on Him. I don't know what hard time you are in now or that you will be facing in the future, but I do know from firsthand experience, God can be trusted, and He is faithful even when life circumstances go completely differently than you planned.

This past year has been a growing year for me, and I truly feel closer to God than ever before. My new passion is reading books that encourage me and challenge me, and God has been asking me to share what I am learning with others. So I have decided to start a blog called "Heartbreak to Strength: sharing what God is teaching me in the midst of my pain."

Please feel free to forward this to anyone going through a hard time; I truly want my vulnerability to encourage others.

Love, Jodi

I still remember how scary this was for me. After I sent out the email, I jumped into the shower. As the water was streaming over my head, I thought, *Oh, crap! What did I just do?*

I raced back to my computer when I was done to see if anyone had responded. I was overwhelmed with what I read.

The replies were beautiful and honest.

Tears streamed down my face as I read about their struggles and difficulties. I was so surprised by their vulnerability. Some told me about problems that they had not told many people. Others thanked me for my honesty. All were sharing something very personal with me that I know I would have never heard if I had not been vulnerable first.

I sat there in awe as I witnessed firsthand the power of vulnerability.

Even though that day was highly emotional, it was a significant one I will never forget. God taught me an important lesson. You will connect deeper with someone through your struggles and hard times than you ever can in your strengths and good times.

Vulnerability breeds connection—deep connection.

Vulnerability breeds connection—deep connection.

When we see someone being authentic, it truly grabs at our hearts. Most people are trying to look like they have it all together. Just scroll through social media like Facebook and Instagram where people are posting their filtered, flawless pictures. Everyone looks like they have perfect lives. No one is sharing their struggles, their pain, or their hard times.

This is what makes vulnerability so rare yet so powerful. When you are authentic, you allow other people to feel comfortable to share their struggles and pain instead of just pretending nothing is wrong.

What is God asking you to share? I am not telling you to email it out to everyone you know, but you can reveal it to a close friend. Imagine what could happen if you removed your mask of perfection, risked being vulnerable, and shared the honest, authentic you?

I believe God will use you in ways you never knew possible. We all have a story, so don't be afraid to use it to connect with others on a deeper level. You never know whose life you will touch and help by being vulnerable!

Speaking of that, here is Part 2 of "Vulnerability." I sent this out a couple of years after my first email.

> I am a single mom to two amazing boys, but if I am completely honest, many times, being a single parent is super hard. I second-guess my parenting all the time, and I feel frustrated that all the responsibility falls on

me. I have an amazing support group that I can turn to for advice and help, but the truth is that I am the only parent in my home, and that can feel overwhelming at times. I try to be an intentional parent, and that takes time. Trying to balance everyone's schedules and mine is challenging. Some days, I feel like I am running around crazy, and most days, I collapse into bed exhausted. I think many of you can relate.

Interestingly, this struggle of being a single mom has made me rely more and more on my faith and dependence on God. When we are weak, He is strong, and I truly believe this. You see, the divorce was heartbreaking and difficult for our family, and I would not wish it on anyone. However, it stretched me and grew me in ways I had never been stretched before. My faith is stronger now than the 2 1/2 years ago that I wrote to you all the first time. I call this the bless in the mess! Some people call it beauty in the ashes.

Just like before, the responses were eye-opening. In *Daring Greatly*, Brené Brown says, "Our rejection of vulnerability often stems from our associating it with dark emotions like fear, shame, grief, sadness, and disappointment. But vulnerability is also the cradle of the emotions and experiences that we crave. It is the birthplace of love, belonging, joy, courage, empathy, and creativity."[34] This is so true.

I know it is hard and scary to be vulnerable, but God has shown me with each genuine email that vulnerability breeds connection.

Friend, do you want deeper connections? Do you want to experience true belonging? It starts with being authentic and honest with those around you. I encourage you to give vulnerability a try and reach out to one friend today. I'm excited for you to connect on a deeper level.

Let's Pray

> *God,* I do not want to forget the truth that others will connect with me more in my struggles than in my strengths. Help me be vulnerable and honestly share my story, my God story, of how You met me in my pain to give me strength, comfort, and hope. Remind me of Your grace when shame rears its ugly head. God, I want real, genuine relationships, so allow me to remember that vulnerability breeds connection. In Jesus's name, Amen."

Truth

> Remove your mask of perfection, risk being vulnerable, and share the honest, authentic you!

16

Offering Forgiveness

Be kind and compassionate to
one another, forgiving each other,
just as in Christ God forgave you.
Ephesians 4:32

I could not believe God was asking me to write another letter to him.

As I cracked open my eyes, all I could see was darkness. The faint light coming off my clock read 5:00 a.m. Wishing I could just roll over and go back to sleep, I knew I needed to get up. This early morning wake up was not random. God had woken me up at dawn on Christmas Day so that I would have time to do what He had asked me to do.

The past two weeks had been the busiest time of the entire year. With presents to wrap, cookies to bake, and lights to hang, the month of December carried with it a huge to-do list. Then God added another item to the already full list. Not excited about what He requested, I agreed, but begrudgingly added, "Only if I have time."

On Christmas Eve, family and friends had filled my house for our annual fondue tradition. We all ate way too much bread with cheese, shrimp, and chocolate-covered strawberries. Laughter from the kids and conversation among the adults had lasted until late in the evening.

After we had said our goodbyes, the night was full of dishes to be washed, stockings to be filled, and gifts to be wrapped. Like a hard-working elf, I had completed my job of being Santa—all alone. With no minutes to spare, I collapsed into bed well after midnight.

Now, after I woke up at God's prompting, the house was quiet and still. In my pitch-black bedroom, I propped up my tired body and slipped out of bed. Even with the sleep deprivation, I knew it was time to do what God had said. Sitting down at my desk, I clicked on my computer and stared at the blank screen.

With my boys fast asleep, I began writing a letter of forgiveness to their father.

It has been almost two years since the night my world came crashing down and my marriage ended. During that time, I had been working on getting to a place where I could truly forgive. Knowing I did not want to stay stuck in bitterness and resentment, I had read books on the subject as well as discussed it weekly with my counselor.

As I started to understand forgiveness more, I realized it was not a one-time thing. Daily, I had to turn over my hurt, disappointment, and anger to God and ask Him to give me the strength to forgive. As I forgave, I had come to a place of freedom—and it was from this place that God was asking me to write to the man who had so deeply hurt me.

Honestly, I tried to pretend that I did not clearly hear God's directions. I even told my friends that I was not sure if this was exactly what He wanted me to do. When I had told God, "Only if I have time," I was attempting to be obedient but also find a way to stall.

If I can be completely vulnerable with you, I knew what God had clearly asked me to do from the beginning. I just did not want to do it.

My pride was getting in the way of my obedience. God wanted me to humbly share, and I wanted to run the opposite way. For the first time, I understood how Jonah felt when God asked him to go to Nineveh, and he bolted the other way on a boat. Just like Jonah, I did not want to extend grace.

If you are unfamiliar with the story, Jonah did not believe the city of Nineveh deserved God's grace, so he ran from the clear directions God had given him. Ending up on a ship in a huge storm, he realized he could not outrun the Lord. He jumped into the water to save the crew on board, was swallowed by a whale, and was delivered by God so he could follow the original directions to go to Nineveh (Jonah 1–3).

Learning from Jonah's mistake, I decided to be obedient and follow God's prompting. While my boys snoozed in their beds, I typed away on my computer. It took many attempts to get the words arranged just the way I knew God needed them to be.

Little did I know that this gift of forgiveness was more for me than for my ex-husband.

Later that day when I gave him the letter, neither his response nor his reaction really mattered. The forgiveness letter was about freeing me—freeing me of anger and resentment as I wrote from a place of freedom in God!

God knew this act of obedience would help me experience the full freedom of forgiveness.

The same is true for you. Has someone deeply wronged you? Do you feel like God is asking you to offer forgiveness? I understand how difficult it is to extend grace, but God's instructions to forgive are more about freeing you than the person who hurt you.

I realize now that the letter was never about him. It was about my growth and my release from bitterness.

I believe this truth applies to you too. Your act of obedience will release you from your feelings of resentment.

Offering forgiveness is a gift to your heart more than it is to others.

I know this is not easy. I think one of the hardest things in life is to forgive someone who has deeply hurt you. I know I struggled with it. Maybe you feel like if you forgive this person, then you are saying that what they did to you is okay. But forgiveness does not mean you agree with what they did. Instead, it is about relinquishing the bitterness inside you about what they did.

Perhaps they never asked you for forgiveness, and you are waiting until they apologize. But what if they never ask? Do you want your healing to be linked to their choice? The longer you wait to extend grace, the more resentment will build up inside of you and the longer you will suffer.

Maybe everything in your body wants to scream, *They don't deserve it!* You are right; they don't. But honestly, we don't either. You do, however, deserve to experience freedom and heal.

Forgiveness is the path to experience freedom from hurt.

Look at what Sheila Walsh says about forgiveness in her book *The Storm Inside*. "Satan would love to keep each of us in a prison of unforgiveness, bound forever to the one who sinned against us. The enemy has many finely honed darts aimed at the hearts of all who love God—but hear this: he has nothing in his arsenal to combat forgiveness!"[35]

I love that Satan is at a loss as we choose to forgive and give grace to someone that has wronged and hurt us. Not only are we freeing ourselves from bitterness and resentment, but we are sucker punching Satan at the same time. Now, that is amazing.

Forgiveness is not a one-time thing. Instead, it is a daily act of laying your hurt and pain at the feet of Jesus,

Remember, forgiveness is not a one-time thing. Instead, it is a daily act of laying your hurt and pain at the feet of Jesus and asking for strength to relinquish it.

In her book *Forgiving What You Can't Forget*, Lysa TerKeurst says, "Forgiveness is both a decision and a process. You make the decision to forgive for the facts of what happened. But then you must walk through the process of forgiveness for the impact those facts have had on you."[36]

Learning this truth set me free. I can have my marked moment in time that I forgave, and I can expect there will be other impacts that will require me to offer forgiveness again. I pray this truth liberates you too.

Perhaps you are still struggling with offering forgiveness, and you are not sure if you have the strength to do it. Honestly, I don't think we are capable of forgiving in our own power. We need to ask for God's grace and strength to be able to surrender the pain and offer true forgiveness.

Praying for God's power to help you forgive will change the trajectory of your life. My hope is that you can see forgiveness in a new light. Lysa describes it as "a complicated grace that uncomplicates my blinding pain and helps me see beautiful again."[37]

Friend, I want you to see beautiful again! I don't want you to stay stuck in your pain as you hold onto anger. I want you to experience the freedom that comes from offering forgiveness.

Let's Pray

> *God*, You know the pain I have experienced and the hurt I am still feeling. By Your power and strength, help me move to a place of forgiveness where I can lay these hurts and pains at the foot of the cross. Meet me where I am and help me take the next step, whether it is to begin to entertain the thought to forgive or daily surrendering it to You. God, thank You that I can do all things through Christ who gives me strength. Thank You for Your unconditional love and comfort through these hard times. In Jesus's name, Amen."

Truth

> Daily choose to let go and not hold on to the anger and hurt, but give it to God instead.

Seek God and invite Him into your pain.

Tearfully allow yourself time to grieve and process the emotions.

Replace your finite view with God's infinite perspective.

Embrace God's character development in the midst of the chaos.

Never lose sight of God's grace.

Give praise to God even as your heart breaks.

Trust God is good when your mind is doubting and you don't understand.

Honestly share your story and help another hurting heart.

17

Change Your Focus

Always be joyful. Never stop praying.
Be thankful in all circumstances,
for this is God's will for you
who belong to Christ Jesus.
1 Thessalonians 5:16–18 NLT

I felt like I had a deep hole in my heart.

Another holiday morning before dawn, my eyes opened just minutes before my alarm buzzed. For most of the night, I had been up every hour checking the time on my clock. Today was an important day, and I did not want to oversleep and miss my scheduled video call with my early risers.

Only seven and eleven years old at the time, my boys had left the day before to travel up north with their dad to spend Thanksgiving with his side of the family. As they were saying goodbye, they promised me they would call me as soon as they woke up the next morning.

Prone to wake up before the sun, my kids were usually my alarm. Today, however, they were not with me.

Instead, I had to rely on the digital clock on my nightstand.

Still completely dark outside, the light shone 6:00 a.m. I knew they would be calling any minute. I got up and went down the pitch-black hall to grab my phone from the charger. As I walked down the corridor of my empty house, it was painfully silent. *I wish my kids were home. I already miss them so much.*

Just as I removed the charger cord, the phone rang. *It's them!* I gladly answered their video call and stared at the black screen. The boys had kept the light off in their room, so they wouldn't wake their dad and grandparents. Yet even though I could not see my boys, I could hear the sound of their precious voices.

Their sweet giggles and words warmed my heart as we talked in the dark during those early morning hours on Thanksgiving morning. I will never forget that special call because it was our first big holiday away from each other after the divorce. I was grieving both their absence and the recent end of my marriage.

We talked for over an hour that morning. As the sun rose, I could finally begin to see their cute faces appear on the screen as the light shone through the window in their room. My youngest was sad that I could not be there with them, but I assured both boys they were going to have a wonderful day with their cousins and family up north.

I put on a brave smile for them, but deep in my heart I kept thinking, *How am I going to make it through this day?*

Have you ever asked yourself that same question? I believe that some days are more difficult than others during the grief process.

The empty chair at the Christmas table.

The empty crib on Mother's Day.

The empty car seat on the way to Thanksgiving dinner.

Time apart from loved ones is hard, but holidays and special days without your loved ones are the hardest.

Maybe you are struggling with infertility, and your aloneness is a painful reminder that someone is missing from your family.

Perhaps the reality of sharing your kids seems too much to bear. It could be you are by yourself for the first time since a loved one has passed, and you deeply miss them. If this describes you, let me be the first to say that I am so sorry.

During those super hard days, I recommend surrounding yourself with people who love you and can cry with you when you are hurting. You want to be around others who can empathize with you and help you get through the rough times.

Waking up on a national family day without my family was one of my most difficult days after my divorce.

There were lots of tears that first Thanksgiving without the boys. It helped to hear their laughs and cheery voices that morning through the phone, but it was still not the same as having them there with me. I spent the rest of that day with my sisters. My oldest one loved to cook, so she prepared a delicious meal at her home. Even with the wonderful food and great conversation, my heart still longed for my two kids.

That afternoon as my sisters and I were cleaning up the dishes, I received a text with a movie of my younger son doing a magic trick. It was wonderful to see his performance, but it was another vivid reminder that I was not with him. I started to realize all that I was missing. Not only was I missing memories with my boys, but time with my nieces and nephews, whom I loved dearly, and conversation with my sister-in-law and mother-in-law. One of the worst parts of divorce is how it severs those extended family relationships.

I called a friend that evening after I got home from dinner with my sisters and just cried with her. The void that penetrated my heart was *that* real. I had barely made it through the day. I honestly just wished the day would be over.

When we are alone and isolated from those we love, it can make us think everything is bleak and hopeless. During these times, it is easy to see only the negative. We get focused on what we have lost, and it is hard to see past it.

The next morning, God shared some truth with me through a devotional by Pastor Rick Warren. God's timing was perfect for me to hear exactly what I needed during my pain. Called "Trusting God through Gratitude," the devotional's message touched my hurting heart.

> How does gratitude develop my faith? It happens when times are tough—when things don't make sense, when you can't figure it out, when your prayers are unanswered, when everything is going the way you didn't want it to go. It happens when you can say in those circumstances, "God, I know you're in control. I know you love me, and I know you can bring good out of this. I'm thankful that you're bigger than my problem."[38]

Here's my favorite part. "That is the ultimate test of the depth of your faith. Can you thank God when life stinks? When you're going through tough times, don't look at what's lost. Look at what's left and be grateful for it!"[39]

I realized that the day before, I had focused on what I had lost. I was grieving my first big holiday without my kids, and I could only see what was missing. But God was reminding me to look at what was left. There were many things I could focus on and be grateful for even in the middle of my loss.

That new way of looking at things changed my life.

I stopped reading the devotional and took out my journal. I began to list all the wonderful blessings I still had in my life. Of course, my kids were at the top of the list along with my amazing time with God. I wrote down examples of God's faithfulness in my life during other hard times. I journaled for about an hour, and I thanked God for my friends who were so supportive and encouraging to me and my family who loved me and cared about me.

That simple choice to practice gratitude shifted my entire attitude. Even though my **Even though my circumstances did not change, my perspective did.** circumstances did not change, my perspective did.

I want to encourage you to grab a pen and some paper and start making your own gratitude list. I know this is difficult to do when you are focusing on what is missing in your life. However, I believe Satan would like nothing more than to see you fixated on what is lost instead of the blessings that God has surrounded you with. You can praise Him even when your heart is still empty.

Whatever the reason, your first Thanksgiving, first Christmas, first Mother's Day, and first Father's Day apart from your loved ones will be some of your hardest days, so give yourself lots of grace. Please do not put any expectations on yourself to follow the same traditions you have had in the past. Instead, surround yourself with people who love you and can cry with you when you are hurting. Ask God for strength and energy to get through the day. Invite friends to pray for you too.

Since holidays have a way of magnifying your grief, I created a resource in the back of the book, "Ten Steps to Help You through the Holidays" (see Appendix B). Here are some items from the list that helped me that Thanksgiving weekend apart from my boys.

- Be honest with how you are feeling and let others know what you need.
- Talk about the loved one(s) you are missing.
- Guard your heart by taking a social media break.
- Fill your mind with truth by listening to worship music or reading a helpful book.
- Please don't rush your grief. You set your pace for the day.
- And most importantly, remember that it is okay not to be okay.

Grieving the loss of a loved one is hard, but holidays without your loved one are the hardest. I am praying for you as God helps you get through this difficult time.

As you cry out to Him, I encourage you to use the names of God in the Bible that show His nature. Here are some examples that I recently learned in Melissa Spoelstra's Bible study called *The Names of God*.[40]

- El Roi: The God Who Sees Me
- El Shaddai: The All-Sufficient One
- El Olam: Everlasting God
- Yahweh Shalom: The Lord is Peace
- Yahweh Yireh: The Lord Will Provide
- Yahweh Raah: The Lord My Shepherd.

If we focus on God and His character alone, we can find many things to be thankful for. Thanking God in the middle of your heartbreak will radically change your outlook. It does not take away the painful circumstance, but it will fill your heart with peace, a peace that surpasses all understanding.

Let's Pray

God, I miss my loved ones today. The pain is so real, and I feel like there is a deep hole in my heart. *El Shaddai*, I ask today for Your strength and comfort to get me through the day. I pray that my family and friends will offer their love and support. *Yahweh Yireh*, help me to find things to be grateful for in the middle of my time of loss. *El Roi*, I am thankful that I don't have to walk through this alone. In Jesus's name, Amen..

Truth

Choosing to practice gratitude will shift your entire attitude.

18

Praise Him in Your Storm

Sing out your thanks to the Lord;
sing praises to our God.
Psalm 147:7 NLT

The lyrics touched my heart.

I started up my car to go to the dreaded appointment. I popped in the new music CD, a gift from a friend who had purposefully handpicked different songs by various artists knowing the heartbreak my family was experiencing.

Just two months earlier, my home had changed from four people living under one roof to three. The aftermath of this alteration was still having ripple effects: Raw emotions. Frequent tears. The stress of finding a mediator and divorce lawyer. In addition to the grief and rejection, I also had to educate myself on family law. *How will we divide up our home and finances? Who will get the kids for the holidays?* Such questions had continually bombarded my mind in the weeks that followed our marital split.

Now it was time to meet with my husband and the mediator for the first time to determine how to uncouple our lives. My stomach was in knots as I typed the address into my phone to get directions. *I wish I was headed somewhere else.*

Overwhelmed by the entire process, I had reached out to family and friends specifically requesting them to pray that I would be able to control my reactions and responses during this meeting. Knowing how hard it was going to be, I asked God to give me His peace beyond understanding.

Yet I backed out of my driveway with a heavy heart. I turned up the volume in hopes the CD would help calm my nerves and keep my mind from ruminating on what was to come.

Have you ever noticed how music has a way of penetrating your heart? Sometimes a song's words are exactly what you need to hear. It is like the musician knows precisely how you are feeling, and the lyrics touch you in ways you cannot describe.

That is what happened to me on the car ride—and one song in particular became the answer to my prayers.

Blaring through the speakers was the Casting Crowns song "Praise You in This Storm."[41] Captivated by its words about praising God and feeling His presence and compassion even when our hearts are torn, I decided to listen to it again. As the lyrics soothed me, I pushed repeat again! The third time around, I started singing it loudly in my car—and by the fourth time, my left arm was in the air as I belted out how God never left my side!

I don't know if any other drivers looked over and saw me, but I bet they would have wondered what was going on it the car next to them if they had.

Worshipping God through that song gave me peace. With each lyric, I surrendered my entire situation to Him.

Voice raised.

Tears down my cheeks.

Fully letting it go to God.

In the midst of my storm, heading to the mediator's office to meet with my husband to discuss our divorce, I was truly able to praise the Lord! I started out anxious and nervous, but now there was a stillness, a calm, over me.

I cannot fully explain how powerful that moment was for me. Nothing had changed externally—but everything had changed internally.

During that thirty-minute drive, God completely shifted my perspective. What began with worry over how to split up our lives ended with peace, knowing God was in control. I did not need to have all the answers. I just needed to trust the One who does.

Where do you need to invite God's peace into your life through praising His name? Maybe you are questioning, *How can I offer Him praise while I am enduring my difficult circumstances?*

Friend, you are not thanking God for your heartbreak, your grief, or your pain. Instead, you are praising God for who He is.

The God who loves you, sees you, and walks through the storm with you.

The God whom you can fully trust and lean on when you are alone and hurting.

The God who cares deeply for you and wants you to grow deeper in your faith.

That is why you can praise Him.

Let me be clear. This is not the same as living in denial. Like I shared in previous chapters, it is important to tearfully allow yourself time to grieve. I am a firm believer in counseling and finding support groups so you can walk through the pain. But at the same time, I also know the power of thanksgiving in the middle of the difficult emotions.

Offering gratitude will always shift your attitude, and that perspective change is key.

Do you see a blessing in the middle of your burden?

Are you able to lift your hands when things are still unclear and messy, when your heart is still broken?

Can you truly give thanks when the waves of grief seem so close together that you are being knocked down and can barely get your head above water?

Do you really believe it is possible to truly praise God in the middle of the storm?

Honestly, before that car ride, I might have said no, but after feeling God's presence over me, I can confidently say yes. God showed me it is possible with His strength, not my own. With God's help, all things are possible. That doesn't mean they will be easy.

I cannot count how many times I played that song by Casting Crowns on repeat whenever the heartbreaking realities of divorce threatened to knock me down. I listened to it again when my friend was diagnosed with cancer. I am sure I will need to hear it yet again when my next storm comes blazing through.

I believe God strengthens you through worship! As you release your worries and stresses with hands raised high and thank Him for who He is, He fills you with His power and peace in the middle of it all.

As I am revising this chapter, it is just days before Thanksgiving, and my pastor just preached a message called "How God Blesses Grateful Hearts." He shared that one of the ways we express gratitude is by singing back to God. Together as a church family, we sang a montage of worship songs that centered on thankfulness. The timing of completing this chapter with the revelation of the truth shared in that service is not lost on me.

Friend, there is power in singing and giving God praise even as your heart breaks. I listened intently to the lyrics of the songs used in that service. Some encouraged us to lift our hands. Others talked about singing in the middle of the storm. All of them focused on giving thanks to our faithful God!

Let me share with you some of these song titles so you can add them to your list of praise songs to sing back to God. I also added a couple of my favorites that help me worship Him.

- "Raise a Hallelujah" by Bethel Music
- "Give Thanks" by Don Moen
- "We Thank You" by Saddleback Worship
- "The Lord our God" by Kristian Stanfill
- "Blessings" by Laura Story
- "Just Be Held" by Casting Crowns
- "Into Dust" by Mack Brock
- "Soar" by Meredith Andrews

I promise you that listening to these songs and freely singing to God will completely change your attitude.

At that same service, we also participated in communion. The pastor shared how the Lord's Supper is also called the Eucharist, which in Greek means "thanksgiving." Again I stood in awe of God because I had just been studying Ann Voskamp's book, *One Thousand Gifts*, in which she shared something similar about thanksgiving and how it relates to joy.

Ann dug deeper into the original language of some familiar Scripture verses read at communion, specifically Luke 22:19, which speaks of when Jesus gave thanks and broke bread with His disciples the night before His crucifixion. She shared that the words "he gives thanks" is translated from *eucharisteo*. Then she added a nugget of truth about the Greek root word, *chara*—it means joy.

As she found the correlation between joy and thanksgiving, she asked a profound question in her book. "Is the height of my *chara* joy dependent of the depths of my *eucharisteo* thanks?"[42]

I know it is hard to be grateful in the middle of your hard circumstances, but what if that gratitude will ignite joy inside of you? I have always wondered why James said, "Consider it pure joy, my brothers and sisters, whenever you face trials of many kinds" (James 1:2). I don't know about you, but joy is the last emotion that I am feeling.

But what if that joy is linked to praising God and asking Him for His strength to help you persevere? James continued in with these words: "Because you know that the testing of your faith produces perseverance. Let perseverance finish its work so that you may be mature and complete, not lacking anything" (James 1:3–4).

Growth comes from persevering through the storms.

Growth comes from persevering through the storms.

Can you picture your roots growing deeper each time you praise Him in hard times? Each act of trust and surrender will grow your faith and produce perseverance, ultimately leading to spiritual maturity. Calling God good in spite of your situations is one of the most difficult things you'll ever do. But it is one of the most powerful ways God begins to heal you.

Carefully read this truth: "Let your roots grow down into him, and let your lives be built on him. Then your faith will grow strong in the truth you were taught, and you will overflow with thankfulness" (Colossians 2:7 NLT).

I don't know about you, but I want to overflow with thankfulness. I want to be exuberant with joy and be filled with God's powerful peace.

So, let's end with a challenge. I want you to choose a worship song from the ones listed earlier or a personal favorite. Then I recommend blasting it either in your car or your home. I encourage you to let the lyrics sink into you as you lift your hands up high into the air. Play it over and over again. Sing along with it, belting it out at the top of your lungs. Let the emotions flow out of you. With tears streaming down your face, fully give God your praise even in the middle of your pain.

I promise something powerful will happen inside of you.

Let's Pray

> *God*, if I am completely honest, it is hard to show grate-fulness when my heart is breaking. So, I ask You to give me Your strength and help me see my circumstances through a different lens. These difficulties are teaching me dependence on You. Today, I want to worship and sing praises back to You, showing my gratitude for Your faithfulness to walk through this storm with me. In Je-sus's name, Amen.

Truth

> Praising God in the middle of the storm does not change your circumstances, but it will change you.

19

The Gift of a Day

I am suffering and in pain.
Rescue me, O God, by your saving power.
Then I will praise God's name with singing,
and I will honor him with thanksgiving.
Psalm 69:29–30 NLT

I will never forget that day God gifted to me.

"Would you like me to warm you up some soup?" I asked Jeannie as she rested in a special hospital bed placed in the middle of her dining room where the table once sat.

"Yes," Jeannie answered faintly.

As I propped up my friend with a pillow, I was thankful for the schedule change. Originally, I had planned to take our younger kids to a trampoline park so Jeannie could rest without any interruptions. Our older teenagers were away at junior high summer camp, and I knew her body needed the extra sleep.

However, a text from Jeannie that morning changed everything. She asked if I could come to her house instead. She was getting weaker and was concerned about being alone for the day. I told her I would be happy to come and help and made arrangements for the kids to come along but play upstairs.

Little did I know then what a gift that change of my plans would become.

As I warmed up the broth in the microwave, my mind drifted back to her phone call just four months before, the shocking diagnosis, and the uphill battle with the chemotherapy appointments that followed. My friend had fought hard, but sadly, the cancer was winning.

Standing in her kitchen just a couple of footsteps across from her, I glanced over at Jeannie's frail body lying in bed. My heart was breaking as I realized my time with her was fleeting. My friend was dying, and I was not ready to say goodbye. I was not prepared to lose her.

We had supported each other through many hard times, and I had so much to share with her, knowing her time on earth was quickly coming to an end. Honestly, we had engaged in many deep conversations over the past four months, but somehow, I sensed that today was going to be one of the toughest.

The microwave beeped, letting me know the soup was ready. I grabbed a spoon and sat down next to her on the bed. In between each serving, we talked. We laughed. We cried.

I told Jeannie how thankful I was that God had brought her into my life. I shared with her what an amazing friend she was to me, and how I would cherish all our memories. With tears flowing from both of our eyes, I told her I was proud of her and how strong she had been through this. Her faith was inspiring!

I also reminded her that she was leaving behind a wonderful legacy. Both of her kids knew Jesus and were aware of how much their mother loved them. Jeannie was such an intentional mom.

She then shared with me how she was feeling. It had been a tough couple of weeks for her as many of her family and friends came to say their farewells. I sat there listening, struggling with how difficult everything had been for her.

As our conversation turned to talking about her children, our eyes became floodgates as we began to weep. A mother's worst nightmare is that something will happen, and she will not be there to watch her kids grow up and be there for them during their ups and downs. This was becoming a harsh reality for Jeannie, and we were both heartbroken.

I wanted to yell at the top of my lungs, *God, this is not fair! Her kids are still so young, and they need a mother!* But in that moment, I knew Jeannie just needed me to be there for her and reassure her about her children. I promised her that I would be there for both of them. I told her that I could never replace her, but I would help them the best I could.

We shared lots of tears as well as lots of memories that special day. I will always cherish that precious time I had with my friend—a gift in the middle of the most heartbreaking of circumstances. Not everyone gets to share with their loved ones what they meant to them. In my heart, I was praising God for the gift of a day in the middle of the storm.

Suddenly I was reminded of a song that had helped me two years earlier in the middle of my heartbreaking divorce. I ran out to my car to grab the Casting Crowns CD along with other Christian music I frequently played while driving. Even though the circumstances were starkly different, the heartbreak and imminent loss felt the same.

Right there at Jeannie's bedside we began playing the CDs. I wish I could say it was for our enjoyment, but the reason was vastly different. We were listening and picking the songs Jeannie wanted played at her memorial service. Just minutes earlier, when we had finished our tearful conversation about her kids, Jeannie asked, "Will you help me plan my funeral? I don't want my husband and kids to be overwhelmed with the planning." Even in her deepest pain, Jeannie was thinking of others.

With tears gushing down my face, I said, "Yes, I am here for you. I can help with whatever you need."

I put the Saddleback Church Worship CD on first. After sitting together at church each week over the past couple of years, we had gained so many memories attached to those songs. As each one played, I remember thinking, *I am going to miss standing next to my friend and worshipping together.* As we talked and reminisced, Jeannie chose two of our favorites: "Good, Good Father" and "Your Will Be Done." Both seemed fitting for her service.

Next, I grabbed the Casting Crowns CD to share the song that had encouraged me during my divorce. I held her hands, and we wept together through the lyrics. I will never forget listening to that special song with her about trusting God in the raging storm.

The lyrics describing God as the One who gives and takes away pierced my heart. I knew my friend's body was shutting down. Unless God performed a miraculous healing, she was going to die. Why hadn't He stepped in and saved the day? I knew God and His plans were good, but I couldn't understand how Jeannie's death was part of this "good" plan.

Yet as the chorus came on, we lifted our hands into the air. Even though my heart was torn, I wanted to praise God. Praise Him that my friend had such a strong faith. Praise Him for my precious time with her in her final days. Praise Him that soon Jeannie would be free of her pain and suffering and in the arms of Jesus, completely healed and cancer free.

Selfishly, I wanted her on earth, but I knew she was headed home to heaven. Watching Jeannie live in excruciating pain those final weeks was so difficult. It was hard to see a loved one suffering. Even though it was special to say our goodbyes and share how much I cared for her, the reality was her body was in deep agony. But praising God with Jeannie helped me to see things in a new perspective.

Did my circumstances change? No. She was still battling pancreatic cancer, and it was winning.

Was my heart still breaking? Yes. Every day I was torn in two by the thought of losing her.

Did I still question why? Yes. I remained conflicted as to why God had not performed a miracle.

Praising God does not mean you will get all the answers. It does not guarantee a miraculous healing. Outwardly, everything might remain exactly the same. However, praising God changes you inwardly. It fills you with a peace beyond your understanding.

Do you need to be filled with peace? Does your heart need some hope? I encourage you to find one thing to praise God for in the middle of your difficulties. Maybe it is the gift of a day like I experienced with Jeannie. Perhaps it is the gift of a person, a friend who supports you in your hard time. It could be the gift of an encouraging word spoken to you by someone who cares.

Focus on the small gifts God provides in the middle of the big storm. **Offer praise to God even when it does not make sense.** Praise the Lord for His presence, His peace, and His love. I know how tough this can be, but I also know how freeing it is. In the midst of the tears, the sadness, and the pain, offer praise to God even when it does not make sense.

Habakkuk understood the power of praise as he wrote these words:

> Though the fig tree does not bud, and there are no grapes on the vines, though the olive crop fails, and the fields produce no food, though there are no sheep in the pen and no cattle in the stalls, yet I will rejoice in the Lord. I will be joyful in God my Savior. (Habakkuk 3:17–18)

Don't get stuck in the *though* statements. Move through to the *yet*!

A friend encouraged me to rewrite the verse in Habakkuk using my own words. This is what I came up with: "Though my friend is losing her battle to pancreatic cancer, though her young kids still need a mother, though we did not get the miracle we prayed for, yet I will rejoice in the Lord. I will be joyful in God my Savior."

I want to challenge you to write your own version of the Habakkuk verse too. Boldly read it and pray for God to give you His perspective as you rejoice in the middle of your heartbreak. Ask Him to reveal both His presence and the remarkable presents He has provided.

That day with Jeannie, I realized just how precious the gift of time truly was. God gave that to me just two weeks before she passed. I still treasure it with all my heart.

The last week of Jeannie's life, I helped with her kids each day. When I picked them up, I ran into her house, held Jeannie's frail hand in mine, and asked her how she was doing. Struggling to talk, she would share just a few words. I reminded her that I loved her dearly and kissed her on the forehead before I left.

I said my final farewell to her on a Wednesday afternoon after dropping off her kids. She passed away early the next morning. As I spoke at her memorial service, I shared exactly what I told Jeannie that day in her house. I shared about the important legacy she left behind for her kids and loved ones. Then as we sang "Good, Good Father," one of the songs she chose that day, I was reminded once more that God is good, and He loves us very much.

Whenever I hear this song at church, I flash back to singing it at her service. Do you believe that God is a good, good Father? It is easy when life is going well, but do you genuinely trust that it is true when times are tough?

Jeannie wanted people to remember and believe that God is a good, good Father. No matter what happens, He truly cares about you. Jeannie left this world knowing that she was going to meet her good Father in Heaven.

Friend, I encourage you to find your small gift from God in the middle of the storm.

Let's Pray

>*God*, I want to find ways to praise You even in the middle of my heartbreaking circumstances, so I ask You to open my eyes and allow me see the small gifts You have provided. Turn my focus off my problems and onto You. Show me Your eternal perspective and help me to trust You even when I don't understand. In Jesus's name, Amen.

Truth

>Focus on the small gifts in the middle of the big storm. A gift of time, a gift of a friend, or a gift of an encouraging word can change your outlook.

Seek God and invite Him into your pain.

Tearfully allow yourself time to grieve and process the emotions.

Replace your finite view with God's infinite perspective.

Embrace God's character development in the midst of the chaos.

Never lose sight of God's grace.

Give praise to God even as your heart breaks.

Trust God is good when your mind is doubting and you don't understand.

Honestly share your story and help another hurting heart.

20

Why, God?

Trust in the Lord with all your heart,
and do not lean on your own understanding.
In all your ways acknowledge Him,
and He will make straight your paths.
Proverbs 3:5–6 ESV

I did not understand why.

I placed the beautiful bouquet of sunflowers on the center of the stage next to her portrait. Finding a solo headshot of my friend to enlarge for her memorial service had been difficult. Most of Jeannie's photos were with her family. The one I chose and digitally edited zoomed in on her as she smiled ear to ear next to her kids and husband. *She looks beautiful,* I thought as I stared at her picture next to her favorite flowers.

Those yellow petals brightened up the gloomy white tent filled with rows of chairs facing the stage. Soon, I knew those seats would be filled with Jeannie's friends and family. *Today is going to be a heavy day.* I carried the second large vase of sunflowers to the entrance table where her loved ones would sign the guest book as they entered and pick up a program celebrating her life.

The musicians arrived and began to practice singing the songs that Jeannie and I had picked out just weeks earlier. The man running the audio was getting Jeannie's life video ready to play for the service. As pictures of Jeannie with her kids flashed up on the screen, my eyes teared up. *Why did cancer have to rob this family of their precious mom?*

Honestly, I had a lot of *why* questions and conversations with God during the last months of Jeannie's life.

Sitting next to Jeannie's recliner during her chemotherapy treatments, I pleaded with God that the side effects would be minimal, and my friend would not be in pain. I asked God to give Jeannie strength to endure another round each time we went. My deepest desire was that God would miraculously heal Jeannie. I prayed fervently for the Lord to lay His hands on her and restore her to health.

It was hard watching her suffer. I remember crying out to God, almost negotiating with Him. "God, if you cure Jeannie, then others will hear her story and believe in you. People know she is a strong Christian, and her loved ones are praying for her. God, if you miraculously make her well, then I promise you will get all the glory. God, please heal my friend."

Sadly, He did not choose to heal her—and I simply didn't understand. *Why did she have to die so young? Why do two little kids have to grow up without a mom? Why do some people with cancer get healed and others do not?* All those questions and others like them persisted within me.

Maybe you don't understand why either. Perhaps you are asking similar questions about the loss of your loved ones. *Why did God not heal? Why didn't we get our miracle? If God was a good God, why would He let them die?*

It is natural to ask these why questions in the middle of our grief. Even more, I believe God is okay with us asking these hard questions. He can handle our doubts about whether He is still good in the middle of our difficult circumstances.

In Craig Groeschel's book *Hope in the Dark,* he addresses some of these questions. He reveals, "You can doubt, question, and even struggle in your faith. But instead of finding that the questions distance you from the heart of God, you will discover something else, something much better. Honest questions, sincere doubt, and deep hurts can draw you closer to God than you've ever been before."[43]

Could asking our why questions help us know God more intimately? Could our doubts actually strengthen our faith in Him? What if our broken hearts deepen our dependence on the Lord?

As I think back to those hard months when Jeannie was fighting for her life, we were both praying and depending on God like we never had before. Even though He did not answer our prayers the way we wanted, we both felt God's presence in the middle of it all. Even though it did not end like we had hoped, God faithfully walked by our sides.

He is faithful to walk with you during your heartbreak too. He will provide friends and family to support you, cry with you, and help you with daily needs like meals and childcare. He shows up in the smallest of details because He truly cares about you and what you are going through.

The hardest times in your life will become the most growing times in your faith.

The hardest times in your life will become the most growing times in your faith.

As I wrestled to make sense of my why questions, I realized that I probably will not get any answers this side of heaven. However, I concluded that I could choose to fully trust God without fully understanding Him. I could decide to run to God in my pain, even when my broken heart had not completely come to terms with my hurt.

I believe the same is true for you. You can trust God without fully understanding God.

I know you want to wait until you have all the answers. But what if running to God in the middle of your pain *is* the answer? The Lord does not want you to grieve your heartbreak alone. He wants to be by your side—comforting you, helping you, and filling you with His peace.

You may discover that His presence will comfort you more than any answer to your why questions.

Just weeks before Jeannie passed, I remember listening to one of the songs she had chosen for her service as I was driving alone in my car. Jeannie had recently received the news from the doctor that the cancer was still growing despite all the chemo treatments she had endured. I knew in my heart it would take a miracle for my friend to be healed.

To help me cope, I listened to a worship CD from Saddleback Church. Jeannie and I both loved "Your Will Be Done."[44] Song lyrics were once again bringing healing to my soul.

I remember crying out to God and pleading with him to heal my friend. I don't think I have ever prayed so fervently before. With tears streaming down my face, I begged God for a miracle.

I played the song once, then twice. By the third time, I remember singing it at full volume. With tears flowing down my cheeks, I prayed, "God, if it is your will, would you please heal my friend?" Each time the song repeated, I boldly said it louder. "God, if it is your will, would you please heal my friend?" By the time I reached my destination, I was sobbing—and as my car came to a stop, I ended with the words, "God, your will be done." My perspective had shifted, and my trust was in Him alone.

Not surprisingly, I teared up again as I heard that same song at Jeannie's memorial service. The chorus is based on Isaiah 55:8–9. "'For my thoughts are not like your thoughts, neither are your ways, my ways,' declares the LORD. 'As the heavens are higher than the Earth, so my ways are higher than your ways and my thoughts than your thoughts.'" As you pray for God's will to be done, you can let go of control especially when life is out of your hands.

The words, *Your will be done,* are not easy to say. They involve complete surrender. Letting go of our own desires to embrace and trust God's plans even when they don't make sense is hard.

Jesus Himself had to speak those difficult words the night before He was crucified. In the Garden of Gethsemane, He was praying so fervently that His sweat fell to the ground like great drops of blood (Luke 22:44). His spirit was in deep agony. He kneeled and prayed, "Father, if you are willing, take this cup from me; yet not my will, but yours be done" (Luke 22:42).

Picture this for a minute. Jesus, who was fully God, was also fully human. As a human, in heart-wrenching anguish, He is crying out to His Father. With drops of blood streaming down His face, He prays fervently with all of His strength. Does that sound familiar? It's much like you. Jesus understands just how hard it is to say those words, *Your will be done.*

Can you say those words as Jesus did? "Not my will, but yours be done."

I know it's difficult. Losing a loved one is one of the toughest things to go through. The heartbreak and hurt can be unbearable. Wanting relief from the pain, you search for answers. Hoping they will ease your agony, you ask, "Why, God?" Then, when your questions are left unanswered, it is easy to become frustrated and angry with God. It is common to question His goodness in times of grief. I know. I have been there.

The key is to not stay there.

Don't get stuck thinking God does not love or care about you. It is okay to question things, but don't remain distant from God in the pain. Don't believe the lies that God is not good and He has forgotten about you and your family. The truth is actually the opposite; He is grieving alongside you and walking with you. Remember, "The Lord is close to the brokenhearted" (Psalm 34:18).

I know you feel lost, but keep crying out to God in your heartache.

I know you want to push God away, but keep turning to Him daily.

I know you are questioning whether God hears your prayers, but keep calling out to Him for His amazing comfort and peace.

I do not fully understand why God did not miraculously heal my friend. I do not understand why you did not get your miracle either. But trust God anyway.

In *Hope in the Dark,* Craig Groeschel shares two stories. In one, the family gets the miracle; in the other, the family plans a funeral. He shares this profound truth.

> Some might ask why God was with the first family and not with the second. I hope you can see that God was with them both—simply in different ways. For the first family, God was with them as healer. For the second, He was with them as comforter. Though they experienced one of life's deepest losses, they also experienced one of life's deepest measures of God's grace. He was there for them every moment of every painful day.[45]

This was so eye-opening for me. God was *with* both families. I know many of us would choose God as the healer if we were writing our stories. But now that I have walked three times with God as my comforter, I can confidently say that He is faithful. Not only will He comfort you, but He will strengthen you and daily be with you. Just because He did not answer your prayer like you hoped doesn't mean His presence has left your side.

Friend, each of us reach a crossroads where we need to decide, Is God good all the time, or is God good only when life circumstances are good? Is God faithful all the time or only when my life is going as I hoped and expected?

Sometimes these expectations of what we thought a good God should have done can keep us from trusting that He is working in our lives. Stop believing that lie. Don't allow your questions and doubts to push you away from Him.

Instead, let them draw you closer to your Savior. He has not forgotten you! He wants to wrap His loving arms around you to sustain you. Wrestle with God through the hard questions, yet continue to trust that He is good. I promise you will become stronger in your faith with deeper roots than ever before.

I believe your greatest heartbreak will catapult you to your greatest growth.

Let's Pray

> *God*, thank You that You are working behind the scenes even when I cannot see it. Help me choose to trust You and Your plans for my life even when I don't understand. Remind me that You are good and that You truly care about me despite the hard circumstances I am walking through. Take all my why questions and doubts and allow them to deepen my faith in You. In Jesus's name, Amen.

Truth

> You can choose to fully trust God without fully understanding God.

21

Detours

You intended to harm me,
but God intended it for good
to accomplish what is now being done,
the saving of many lives.
Genesis 50:20

Life took an unexpected turn.

Driving home from the store, I glanced in the rearview mirror at the car seat behind me. Kyle, just three years old, looked out the window with a gloomy gaze. Lately, I had been the one with the sorrowful look as it had only been a couple of months since we lost the baby.

"Are you okay, honey?" I asked with concern.

"I miss the baby," he replied sadly. "I want to send a kiss up to heaven."

Heaven. Who would have thought I would be explaining the afterlife to a toddler? Honestly, this was not how I thought my summer would go. I certainly did not anticipate having such hard conversations with my sweet boy. But the reality was life had taken a detour, an unforeseen curve when I miscarried.

I can think of another person whose life was marked by multiple detours. Let me paint you a picture.

Alone in a pit as the desert heat beat down upon him, my favorite Bible character, Joseph, was exhausted after trying repeatedly to climb out to freedom. Realizing he was stuck there to die, I wonder if Joseph replayed the day's events in his head.

Excited to greet his brothers, he had skipped along wearing his colorful coat. As he got closer, he was not greeted with the smiles he expected, but by angry, determined faces. They had grabbed him, ripped off his coat, and threw him into a pit. Now, as the sun scorched his skin, he thought once more, *Why did they leave me here?*

Tired and confused, Joseph sat all alone and hopeless—until he heard something from above. As the sounds got louder, he was elated to recognize some of the voices. He jumped up, heart pounding with excitement, "Have my brothers returned to rescue me?" But his delight quickly changed when he understood what was really happening.

His brothers were selling him as a slave. Fresh rejection surged through him. "Why are you doing this?" he screamed. "I am your brother." They sneered at him with hatred and rage as Joseph was pulled out of the pit, tied up, and dragged away. As he stumbled along with his captors, Joseph thought, *This is not how I thought my life would end up.*

As I read the Bible, I like to envision what others are feeling and thinking. Can you imagine how painful this must have been for Joseph? As I put myself in his heartbroken shoes, I can see both tears and anger as he felt completely betrayed by his own flesh and blood. This began a series of difficulties for Joseph.

Storms can feel like detours in your life. You are headed one way, and then life takes an abrupt twist onto a path you never asked to be on.

This new trail is lonely.

This unwanted road is harder.

This course you never asked for usually involves loss and grief.

Joseph knew this all too well as he went from the pit to Potiphar's house to prison. Eventually, after fifteen years, he would make it to the palace. Now that is one long detour.

In his book, *Detours*, Tony Evans discusses how these unanticipated routes can actually take us in another, better direction. He says, "Detours are designed for our own good, regardless how we view or feel about them. They are good things that often feel bad. This is because it's in our detours that we're developed for our destiny."[46]

Our character is matured in these alternate routes. Even though they feel frustrating or negative at the time, God is developing us to match our calling. We are learning patience, gratitude, compassion for others, and how to live fully dependent on God.

What if this change was the path God intended you to be on all along?

What if this new direction leads you to your purpose?

What if your success is contingent on your growth as you embrace the diversion?

Looking at detours in a different light helps us see God's bigger perspective.

Looking at detours in a different light helps us see God's bigger perspective.

Let's explore Joseph's story in Genesis chapters 37–50 and see how God used these divine deviations to develop Joseph.

When we first meet Joseph, he is a prideful young man bragging to his brothers about his coat of many colors and sharing his dreams of them bowing down to him.

As someone who has been working on self-awareness for many years, I would say Joseph was completely unaware that his boasting was causing his brothers to become jealous.

Do you think this young, not self-aware Joseph could be en-
trusted with being second in command to the pharaoh? If he would
have been given his destiny at this immature, prideful age, would
he have been successful? We can agree that he clearly was not ready
and therefore would have failed. Joseph needed to grow up—cue
the detours.

Joseph's brothers, in an act of jealousy, threw him into a pit
and sold him as a slave. Heartbroken from his own siblings' deceit,
Joseph arrived in Egypt and was bought once again, ending up at
Potiphar's house. Genesis 39:2 (NLT) says, "The Lord was with Joseph, so he succeeded in everything he did as he served in the home
of his Egyptian master."

That saying, "The Lord was with Joseph," appears multiple
times in the book of Genesis. These words remind us that God is
with us in the middle of our detours too. Just as He did not leave
Joseph, He does not abandon you.

Tony Evans wrote, "One thing to learn from God being with
Joseph is that Joseph was also with God. In other words, Joseph
did not allow the circumstances to compromise his spiritual relationship."[47] Joseph could have been bitter and angry at God for the
many detours, but instead he chose to draw near to Him. It would
be beneficial to follow Joseph's example. He ran after God with his
whole heart and never let the unforeseen hardships affect his close
relationship with the Lord.

As God's hand of favor was over Joseph, Potiphar noticed and
put Joseph in charge of his entire household. Sadly, Potiphar's wife
noticed Joseph too and started to stir up trouble. The Bible says in
Genesis 39:6 that Joseph was a very handsome and well-built man.
No wonder he caught the eye of Potiphar's wife. (This is where I
wish our Bibles had pictures. Oops. I am getting distracted. Sorry
for the detour—pun intended).

Potiphar's wife began to look at Joseph lustfully and pursued him day after day to sleep with her. Each time, Joseph refused. But the woman was relentless and did not give up. Finally, she caught Joseph alone in the house, grabbed his jacket, and demanded he have sex with her. Joseph tore himself away but left his cloak in her hands as he ran from her. Spurned, Potiphar's wife falsely accused him of trying to rape her, and Joseph was cast into prison. Once again, he was taken on another detour.

At this point, Joseph must have been feeling extremely frustrated. After several repeated invitations by Potiphar's wife, he knew he did the right thing by not giving in to the temptation to sleep with her. But now he finds himself incarcerated for a crime he never committed.

That does not seem fair. If I were Joseph, I would have been incredibly angry and discouraged. But look at Genesis 39:21 (NLT): "But the Lord was with Joseph in the prison and showed him his faithful love. And the Lord made Joseph a favorite with the prison warden." I cannot imagine the warden favoring Joseph if he was constantly complaining and bitter about what had happened to him.

Do you see how God transformed and refined Joseph through each difficult circumstance? Again, the Bible says that the Lord was with Joseph in prison. But I think the opposite was true too. Joseph was with God. Instead of holding on to resentment and anger, Joseph ran to God in his pain. Can you see why he is one of my favorite Bible characters? I love watching God's character development unfold in his life. He continually sought God, and God continually grew Joseph.

In jail, Joseph interpreted the dreams of the pharaoh's cupbearer and his chief baker. Joseph also asked the cupbearer to not forget him. "Please remember me and do me a favor when things go well for you. Mention me to Pharaoh, so he might let me out of this place" (Genesis 40:14, NLT). Sadly, the cupbearer did forget Joseph, but God didn't. In His perfect timing, two full years later, Joseph would be brought in front of the pharaoh to interpret his dream.

The Bible is silent on what happens in Joseph's life during that two-year pause. I can only imagine Joseph felt forgotten and overlooked. He was probably confused and asked God, *Where are you? What are your plans for my life? Why am I still here in prison?*

The waiting times in life are hard, especially when you don't always understand why. If you are in the middle of a holding pattern right now, I encourage you to follow Joseph's example of trusting God during the delay.

Why? When God is ready to move, it will happen suddenly. I love that Genesis 41:14 (NLT) says, "Pharaoh sent for Joseph at once, and he was quickly brought from the prison." Some versions say "immediately" or "hastily." Pharaoh did not waste any time, but he swiftly summoned him to interpret his dream.

Joseph then told Pharaoh there was going to be seven years of great prosperity followed by seven years of famine. He recommended that Pharaoh find a wise and intelligent man to oversee the land. "Pharaoh said to Joseph, 'Since God has revealed the meaning of the dreams to you, clearly no one else is as intelligent or wise as you are. You will be in charge of my court, and all my people will take orders from you. Only I, sitting on my throne, will have a rank higher than yours'" (Genesis 41:39–40 NLT).

Joseph was *now* ready to fulfill his purpose! God's timing is always perfect! The years of detours had developed His character to match His calling.

From the betrayal of his brothers to being thrown into a pit.

From the lonely hole to being sold into slavery.

From bondage to being purchased by Potiphar.

From being falsely accused by his wife to being thrown into prison.

From years behind bars to finally reaching the palace so he could rescue His people.

Tony Evans teaches, "God is not going to bring your destiny to fruition until He knows that you are able to handle it spiritually, emotionally, and physically. If you cannot handle it, you will lose it rather than use it for His glory. That is why He focuses so intently on our development as He takes us to our destiny."[48]

Joseph's destiny was to save a nation during a time of famine. Along the way, he learned humility, patience, compassion, forgiveness, and grace—all important lessons to prepare him for his greater purpose. Little did he know then that those lessons would also be needed years later when he saw his brothers again. In search of food, his siblings came to Egypt during the famine, and once again, Joseph came face-to-face with the brothers who betrayed him.

This time, Joseph was a completely different man. The young teenager who bragged about his colorful coat and dreams had been transformed into a mature and humble adult. In one of the most beautiful examples of forgiveness and grace anywhere, Joseph looked into the eyes of his brothers and declared, "You meant evil against me, *but* God meant it for good in order to bring about this present result, to keep many people alive" (Genesis 50:20 NASB).

What a powerful transformation Joseph went through as he walked through those difficult times.

Through each obstacle, Joseph made a choice to trust God even when he did not understand. He believed God had a perfect plan and was in complete control even when his circumstances spiraled out of control.

Like Joseph, I pray you can have this same perspective.

Friend, God has not abandoned you. It is quite the opposite. God is growing you.

He is beginning to chisel away and refine you through the hard times you are experiencing. These delays can last longer than expected and leave you feeling alone and hopeless. But what if God has you on a different route to prepare you for your calling? I pray we can trust that God is good, and so are His plans.

I want to close with a quote from Randy Frazee's book, *The Heart of the Story*.

> No matter how painful some moments seem; your story is not over. If you love God and align your life to his Upper Story purposes, everything in your life, the ups and downs, the mountaintops and valleys, the highs and the lows, the raises and the rejections, the good and the bad are all working together to accomplish good. Be patient. Trust God. Let him mold you during the difficult seasons to equip you for the assignment ahead.[49]

Let's Pray

> *God*, help me see the obstacles in my life the way Joseph did. With each delay and setback, He leaned in closer to You. I want to move in nearer to You in the middle of my unexpected turns. Give me Your perspective and allow me to trust You, even when it does not make sense. Thank you for Joseph's story in the Bible and the lessons we can learn from him. In Jesus's name, Amen

Truth

> Trust that the detours in your life are developing your character to match God's purpose for your life.

22

His Timing, Not Ours

I prayed for this child,
and the LORD has granted me
what I asked of him.
1 Samuel 1:27

I could not believe His perfect timing.

Gazing up at the sky, we watched the four pink balloons float and drift up to heaven. From the park across the street from my house, my family observed them rising higher and higher as they flipped and turned. Ironically, three of the balloons stayed together, and one drifted off all by itself. We stood there in awe as the balloons seemed to symbolically retell our story from when we lost our sweet baby.

I cannot believe it has already been a year. Without making an appearance on earth, my little one had slipped into heaven the previous summer and left us all heartbroken.

Desiring to understand why our baby had stopped growing, we did some genetic testing that summer. The results revealed that our precious baby was a girl. Sadly, she passed away due to Turner's syndrome, a condition where females are missing their second X chromosome. Sometimes referred to as XO, they have only forty-five chromosomes instead of the normal forty-six. Most pregnancies with this disorder end in the first trimester. But because a small percentage of the babies do survive, it is not uncommon to have a second or third trimester loss.

Finding out our baby was a girl, we decided to name her Grace Linzey Rosser. Even though she was only in my womb a short time, she graced us with her swift presence, and she would never be forgotten. The name Grace is also a special family name. Her middle name, Linzey, is in honor of the doctor who helped me with my surgery when everyone else had given up (I shared that story in Chapter 4).

Now was Baby Grace's first Remembrance Day. In honor of the special day, we all took turns writing heartfelt messages on the pink balloons before we released them. The beautiful idea came from our Empty Arms grief support group. We felt it was a great way to recognize her life. In thick black ink, we wrote, "We miss you, Baby Grace. You are loved, Baby Grace. We will never forget you, Baby Grace!"

I am not going to lie; it was an emotional day. The first anniversary of any loss is always hard.

Standing in the middle of the green grass and surrounded by loved ones, I was thankful my parents and sister had come to join us. My husband was holding Kyle, and I was pushing our baby stroller. Conor, only three weeks old, was quietly asleep, oblivious to our special day for his sister.

We kept watching until the balloons had risen completely out of sight. Just like our Baby Grace, they had faded out of our physical sight but would always remain in our hearts and minds. As we said our goodbyes to family, I kept thinking of the roller coaster of emotions from the past year: We lost our baby in June and were gifted with our second son a year later. Reflecting on it all, I remembered back to the crazy day I found out I was pregnant with Conor.

September had just begun, and I could not keep it together emotionally. For several consecutive days I was a crying mess. My mom even said to me, "Honey, you are either pregnant or you need to see a counselor." Thinking maybe I should call a therapist, I decided to take a pregnancy test first. Truthfully, having another child was not on my radar. I was still grieving the loss of Baby Grace.

Looking at the stick, I could see the tiniest glimpse of a second line. My mom's hunch was right. I was expecting again. I don't think I have ever been as scared to death and super excited all at the same time as I was that day. *What if it happens again? What if I lose this baby?* Anxious thoughts swirling in my mind, I called my doctor's office to set up an appointment.

Surprisingly, the doctor called me back that evening. Curious if he was calling about my upcoming appointment, I inquired why he had gotten back to me so quickly. He said he had more results from the genetic testing center. Apparently, they had found that a very small percentage of my own blood contained XO cells, just like Baby Grace had. Because of this, he informed me that there was a tiny chance that I could have another baby with Turner's syndrome.

My heart began to beat faster as I revealed to him that I'd just found out I was pregnant. Sensing my stress, he tried to calm me by reminding me that the chance of a problem was exceedingly small. With what-if questions flooding my brain, I hung up and fell to the floor. Kneeling on the tile next to the tub in my bathroom, I cried out to God. "Please, Lord, keep my baby healthy. I don't want to relive that nightmare again."

Do you find the timing ironic? I had literally discovered that morning that I was expecting; then the same evening, I learned there was a possibility I could miscarry again. Needless to say, I would not see God's providential hand until much later.

There was a woman in the Bible who also did not understand

God's timing for her baby. Desperately wanting a child, Hannah struggled that she could not get pregnant. Hannah must have thought God had overlooked her or that He was ignoring her prayers.

Have you ever felt like that? Are you disheartened by the amount of time it is taking God to answer your prayer?

According to 1 Samuel 1:10 (NLT), "Hannah was in deep anguish, crying bitterly as she prayed to the Lord." I can relate to that. In verse 11, she made a vow to God, "O LORD of Heaven's Armies, if you will look upon my sorrow and answer my prayer and give me a son, then I will give him back to you. He will be yours for his entire lifetime." This is a bold prayer—but what makes it even bolder is that she was praying by herself inside the tabernacle. Eli, the priest, even thought that Hannah was drunk when he saw her.

"Oh no, sir!" she replied. "I haven't been drinking wine or anything stronger. But I am very discouraged, and I was pouring out my heart to the LORD" (1 Samuel 1:15 NLT). We can learn so much from Hannah. When we are discouraged

We can cry out to Him knowing He listens to every detail.

and feel like God has forgotten us, we can pour out our heart to Him. We can passionately pray to Him. We can cry out to Him knowing He listens to every detail. We can share our frustrations, disappointment, and fears.

God did not answer Hannah's request immediately. The Bible says that He responded "in due time" (v. 20). We don't know how long that was, but in God's perfect timing, He granted Hannah's request to have a baby. She gave birth to Samuel, and just as she vowed, she brought him to the tabernacle after she weaned him.

She ran into Eli again. "'Sir, do you remember me?' Hannah asked. 'I am the very woman who stood here several years ago praying to the LORD. I asked the LORD to give me this boy, and he has granted my request. Now I am giving him to the Lord, and he will belong to the Lord his whole life.' And they worshiped the Lord there" (1 Samuel 1:26–28 NLT). What I love about Hannah is that she followed through on what she had promised. I can only imagine how hard that must have been. But she did it anyway.

Samuel grew up to become a mighty prophet for God. He anointed King David and shared important news with King Saul. He had a significant role as God's people transitioned from judges to kings. God needed Samuel to be born at a certain time to accomplish His purposes. So Hannah's waiting was all part of a bigger plan. Looking back now, it all makes sense, but at the time, it was hard to understand why God had her wait.

I think this is true for our circumstances too. In retrospect, our waiting starts to make sense. But can we trust God in the middle of the wait? Can we see that God's plans for our life are good? Can we be confident that He is doing something behind the scenes that we don't fully understand and trust in Him?

Friend, I pray we can learn to trust that God will answer our prayers in His perfect timing.

Today, I can see God's providence in when I found out I was expecting Conor. I honestly don't think I would have purposefully tried to get pregnant if I'd known the risk that I could lose a baby a second time. God knew that I would've been struck by fear and given up on having another child. So even though I was not ready, I can see now that God's timing was perfect!

By having me not wait to get pregnant, God was ensuring that we would have another child.

By having Hannah wait to get pregnant, God was ensuring that Samuel was born during the correct time to fulfill His calling.

I will never completely understand God's timing, but I know I can trust Him. If God has you in a season of waiting, I recommend reading Hannah's full story in 1 Samuel 1. Just like she poured her heart out to the Lord, you can do the same. God might not answer your request immediately, but He will when it is the right time.

At our baby dedication for Conor, I chose 1 Samuel 1:27 (NLT), where Hannah says, "I asked the Lord to give me this boy, and he has granted my request." Another version says, "I prayed for this child, and the LORD has granted me what I asked of him" (NIV). With all the praying I had done, it seemed the correct choice as we gave our son to God.

Proverbs 31 Ministries has a great tool to help you study the Bible. It is called the First 5 app. Each morning, you can read a chapter of the Bible and receive added insight to better understand what you are reading.

In the First 5 app for the 1 Samuel study, Lysa TerKeurst said, "God loves us too much to answer our prayer at any other time than the right time."[50] When you are feeling discouraged, remind yourself of that truth.

Let's Pray

God, if I am completely honest, I don't like waiting. It is hard to have a desire in my heart and not see it fulfilled right away. But I know that You are never in a hurry, and You are never late. In Your perfect timing, You will answer my prayer. Help me trust You and Your bigger plan, especially when I am struggling to understand your timetable. In Jesus's name, Amen."

Truth

Keep trusting that God will answer your prayers in His perfect timing.

Seek God and invite Him into your pain.

Tearfully allow yourself time to grieve and process the emotions.

Replace your finite view with God's infinite perspective.

Embrace God's character development in the midst of the chaos.

Never lose sight of God's grace.

Give praise to God even as your heart breaks.

Trust God is good when your mind is doubting and you don't understand.

Honestly share your story and help another hurting heart.

23

Me Too

Praise be to the God and Father
of our Lord Jesus Christ,

the Father of compassion and
the God of all comfort,
who comforts us in all our troubles,
so that we can comfort
those in any trouble with the comfort
we ourselves receive from God.
2 Corinthians 1:3–4

I was amazed by the similarities in our stories.

My phone rang on a hectic Friday morning. Normally, talking with someone on the phone with two little ones was nearly impossible. Luckily, the baby was down for his morning nap, and my four-year-old was actively engaged with his building blocks in our toy room.

"Hello, Allison," I said, excited to have some adult conversation and catch up with my college friend. Immediately, I could tell by her tone as she responded that something was wrong.

My eyes began to tear up as she told me about a woman at her church named Clarissa who had just lost her sweet baby sixteen weeks into her pregnancy. It was all too familiar for me. Just one year before, I had walked the exact same path. Knowing I could understand what the woman was going through, Allison asked, "Jodi, can you reach out to her?"

I quickly answered yes, not fully understanding how much healing was going to come from my choice to help another hurting heart.

As I ended the call, heaviness weighed on my own heart. Remembering the deep sadness I had experienced as all the hopes and dreams for my baby slipped away in an instant, I knew she was encountering those same painful emotions. Hoping my experience could help her not feel alone in the heartbreak, I decided to contact Clarissa by email.

As I sat down at my computer, I struggled with what to say. I am normally not at a loss for words, but this time, I felt unsure of what to write. Asking God to give me insight, I began my message. "I am so sorry for your loss." Then I shared my personal story with her from the summer before. I let her know that I understood what she was going through. "I'm here for you if you ever want to talk or just cry."

That launched an email conversation that continued for weeks. Clarissa was hesitant to completely open up to someone she never had met, so I mostly just told her my story at the beginning. However, as I honestly shared the raw emotions I felt, she felt comfortable to let her guard down and openly tell me what she was feeling. The discussion got deeper and more vulnerable each time we emailed.

It is very comforting talking with someone who has experienced the same heartbreak as you. There is incredible, healing power in the words *me too.*"

They don't take the pain away, but they remind us that we are not alone. They don't change the hard circumstances, but they help us know that someone else fully understands. Even though I was just a little ahead of Clarissa on the path, my story offered her hope.

We communicated literally every day. I began to share with her all the things that helped me: journaling, planting a tree in memory of our Baby Grace, and sending up balloons to heaven on her Remembrance Day. I encouraged Clarissa to write letters to her sweet baby and share all the hopes and dreams she had for him. There is something therapeutic about getting all of our emotions out on paper.

One of my priceless possessions is a baby book I made in honor of Baby Grace. For weeks I had been journaling, so I used all the words I had written and turned it into a memory keepsake. Even though we did not have many pictures to put in her book, I included the ultrasound pictures of her and the "I am going to be a big brother" pictures of my older son that we took at twelve weeks when we thought we were safely out of the first trimester. I still treasure this baby book and look at it each year on Baby Grace's Remembrance Day.

Each idea I shared with Clarissa brought healing to her—and me too. God was wonderfully using me, taking my heartbreak from losing Baby Grace to bring her comfort. I was truly in awe of how God allowed me to help her in her grief just one year after I walked through my own grief. I did not realize it at the time, but God was teaching me an important life lesson.

God never wastes our hurts.

As I looked back to the summer before, I remember searching the internet for books about losing a baby when I got home from that life-changing doctor's appointment. With so many conflicting feelings, I wanted to know I was not alone in my pain. I was grieving the baby I had never got to hold or meet but who nonetheless was still such a big part of my life. I needed to know that my emotions were normal for what I was going through.

As I read through the books, they brought me great comfort to know that someone else had felt the same. There was healing in those books! They showed me the importance of letting myself grieve her life. The hopes and dreams I had for her were some of the biggest losses.

Since these books had helped me along my journey, I hoped they would help Clarissa too. So I decided to send her a care package with some of the same books I had read along with a CD of the song "Glory Baby." The beautiful song about a baby being in the arms of Jesus had truly touched my heart, and I thought it would do the same for her.

Little did I know just how much that care package would mean to my new friend.

My phone rang again, and Allison's name appeared on the screen. She was calling to tell me about Clarissa's funeral service for her baby, and her tone sounded different this time. It was hopeful.

She shared that they played "Glory Baby" at the service. Before it began, the pastor shared how God had brought a woman Clarissa had never met into her life who had experienced a loss of a baby a year before. He revealed what a blessing her words and support had been to Clarissa and her family as they walked through their heartbreaking circumstances. He ended by mentioning that she even sent the song they were about to hear.

I wept as I realized the pastor was talking about me.

Humbled and in awe of the Lord, I realized God never wastes our hurts and pain. It was like He was whispering to me, *I had a purpose for your pain, Jodi.*

He wants to whisper the same words to you. *I have a purpose for your pain,* _____ (Please insert your name).

I love how God never wastes a hurt. He specializes in redeeming our pain to help others. He takes our heartbreaking loss and comforts us, and then He asks us to comfort others who are going through similar circumstances. Honestly, there was a lot of healing for me that summer when I reached out to Clarissa.

Thinking about how God has purpose for our pain, I also realized we were never meant to grieve alone. I love how God brought Jeannie into my life to help me in my time of grief after I miscarried Baby Grace. He used me to help Clarissa in her pain. Coming full circle helped me in my grief cycle. It's exciting to think that God has future plans for Clarissa to come alongside and help another hurting mother.

God also has plans for you. God wants to redeem your hurts and pains and use you. Are you ready to use your story to help another hurting heart?

Are you ready to use your story to help another hurting heart?

Sharing my story with Clarissa that summer was life changing! Two important things happened to me that rerouted my trajectory.

First, God revealed my life verse to me: It's 2 Corinthians 1:3–4—the feature passage of this chapter. After living it out that summer with Clarissa, I knew God wanted me to claim it for myself.

Second, my book ministry began as I started giving books away to family and friends. I regularly hand them out as birthday or Christmas presents. My heart loves to offer hope by passing along a paperback or hardcover by a favorite author to someone going through a difficult circumstance. Since books had been part of my healing, I enjoyed providing them to others, hoping they would find their healing. It all got underway with me sending that first book to Clarissa.

After that, I ordered multiple copies of *Grieving the Child I Never Knew* by Kathe Wunnenberg to pass along to any mom going through a miscarriage or other loss of a baby. In my care package, I again added the song "Glory Baby" and a handwritten note including Psalm 34:18, "The Lord is close to the brokenhearted." I told them that I am so sorry for their loss and let them know that I understood their pain because I had walked a similar path. I basically said to them, *Me too*.

Do you know someone who needs to hear those powerful words? Has God placed people in your life who would be inspired by your story?

God has a purpose for your pain if you will give it to Him to use.

Who needs to hear your *me too*?

Let's Pray

> *God*, I love that You never waste my pain. Thank You for being the ultimate redeemer and bringing purpose to my loss. I don't understand why I have to go through grief. But one thing I am confident in is that You want to use my heartbreaking story to help someone else. Jesus, give me the courage to share how You met me in my pain and to encourage others. In Jesus's name, Amen.

Truth

> God never wastes a hurt. He specializes in redeeming your pain for His purpose

24

Better Together

Though one may be overpowered,
two can defend themselves.
A cord of three strands is not quickly broken.

Ecclesiastes 4:12

I was amazed how much stronger we are when we're linked together.

Just weeks after Jeannie passed, the new school year began. Her loved ones rallied to help support her husband and kids. Friends helped drive her children to and from school. Meals were provided to ease the burden in the evenings. I had her kids over each week for a playdate with my boys and to check in on them emotionally.

The months after Jeannie's funeral showed me the importance of community. That reminded me of a trip my boys and I took to Sequoia National Park a couple of years before.

One of the must-see highlights of living in California is driving to observe the massive sequoia trees. With each curve up the mountain road, our excitement heightened as we got ready to set eyes on the largest tree in the world, the General Sherman.

Standing directly next to the enormous creation allowed us to not only perceive how tall it was but how wide as well. At 275 feet tall with a base diameter over thirty-six feet, it is not the tallest tree in the world, but it is the largest because of its overall volume. Over 2,000 years old, one of its branches is almost seven feet in diameter. That alone is thicker than the trunk of most trees.

Thinking about the tree's gigantic size along with its old age, I thought, *Wow, this tree must have very deep roots.* Surprisingly, I was wrong. The General Sherman, and all the other giant sequoias, actually have a shallow root system.

So, how do these magnificent trees keep standing strong when winds and storms come?

Amazingly, those towers in the forest rely on each other for their strength. Even though their root systems only go down five to six feet, they actually extend 100 feet wide. Even better, the roots interlock with those of the surrounding trees. They do not have depth, but they have width—and in community they grow and intertwine underground. Can you imagine how much stronger they are as they fuse their root systems together?

We can learn something from these incredibly large living things. Just like the sequoia trees need one another, we also need community.

Community is important, especially when we are walking through loss. Vivian Mabuni says in her book *Open Hands Willing Heart*, "Each heartbreak formed a bridge to connecting with others walking similar roads."[51]

I love the visual she presented. When you find yourself on the center of a bridge, there is often someone ahead of you and behind you. There will be times when you need someone to walk across, meet you in middle, and guide you to the other side. There will also be times when you are the one offering help.

So as we navigate through grief together, we have the privilege of offering support and encouragement to one another. That's community in action.

In her book, *Who Holds the Key to Your Heart*, Lysa TerKeurst wrote,

> To walk the path the Lord delights in, we must be willing to let God use the circumstances of our lives to reach out to others. Let's compare our hurts to stones littering our paths. We have a choice to do one of three things with these stones. We can use them to beat ourselves up, making our scars run deeper than they should. We can throw our stones at others, wounding them and making them also feel pain. Or we can use these stones to build bridges for others to walk across from their own darkness and pain into His healing light.[52]

I don't know about you, but I want to build bridges with my stones. I want to use my heartbreak to help another hurting heart.

Lysa adds, "For when we touch the one who needs healing, we touch the heart of the Healer Himself. And when He pours His healing through you to another, God's healing touches you first and as a result you are healed."[53]

Friend, I believe our healing comes full circle when we come alongside another hurting heart, interlock roots, and offer them hope and encouragement in the middle of their storm.

Who do you need to reach out to today and interlock roots with? Who needs to hear your story of how God met you in your pain? Who might be the one to come alongside you to help you when you are hurting?

I genuinely believe empathy and compassion for others are two of the unexpected gifts found in the midst of life's difficulties.

What if we began looking at our storms from the new perspective of community? I love this quote from Christine Caine: "Sometimes when you're in a dark place you think you've been buried, but actually you've been planted."[54] Wherever we have been planted, we can offer life to one another!

What if the circumstances you are enduring are not burying you, but instead growing roots in you? What if they are planting you in the soil so that God can use those roots to interlock and help someone else?

Friend, the storm you are enduring is preparing you for God's plans and purpose for your life.

This new outlook brings me hope. Hope that God does not waste our hurts. Hope that the experiences of our lives can be used to help others who are hurting. I hope it does the same for you.

Let me tell you another story about driving to see a massive tree.

A couple of years ago, I had the privilege to go see the Angel Oak Tree in South Carolina. Just outside of the city of Charleston, this giant tree stands sixty-five feet high and is 300 to 400 hundred years old. Seeing this tree in person was one of the highlights of my trip.

The trunk was enormous, the branches were huge, and the leaves were green and lush. It was truly breathtaking! However, what enthralled me most about this remarkable tree was what was happening underground. To match the strength of those vast branches, I imagined the remarkable depth of the spectacular old oak tree's root system.

As I stood beneath the majestic Angel Oak, I also recognized the need for spiritual depth in my life. I wanted deep roots like those described when the prophet wrote, "But blessed are those who trust in the Lord and have made the Lord their hope and confidence. They are like trees planted along a riverbank, with roots that reach deep into the water. Such trees are not bothered by the heat or worried by long months of drought. Their leaves stay green, and they never stop producing fruit" (Jeremiah 17:7–8 NLT).

What I did not realize then was just months after standing in front of the Angel Oak, God was going to invite me to start a podcast called Depth! Designed to help others grow deeper in their faith and stronger in their relationships, it became a place where people could share their stories of brokenness, heartbreak, grief, and how God met them in their pain. It became a *community* where we encouraged others walking the storms of life.

I want people to see that God will take their greatest heartbreak and catapult them to their greatest growth. Growing deep roots and then interlocking those roots with each other is such a beautiful picture of how God uses our lives. Through sharing our real-life struggles, we declare God's faithfulness through the pain and inspire one another with our words of hope so that no one is wasting their hurt.

Our stories of heartache and grief were never supposed to stop with us, but they are meant to be shared in community to unleash hope.

I was walking through a home decor store a couple years ago when I saw a beautiful piece of artwork. It featured these words: "God can restore what is broken and change it into something amazing. All you need is faith."

I love how Kyle Idleman defines faith in his book *Don't Give Up*. "Faith is confidence that keeps believing all the pieces are going to somehow fit together, even when we don't have the big picture to work from. It's believing that God has a purpose, even when there seems to be no reason."[55] Kyle asks us to wrestle with the question, "Am I following God in a way that requires faith?" He continues, "If your answer is yes, then I have a follow-up question for you: Can you tell me a story?"[56]

You see, we don't share our faith with a long theological answer. We share our faith using our personal testimonies of how God showed up and provided for us when we could only see part of the picture. Kyle says, "A story of faith is almost always a 'don't give up' story of perseverance."[57]

Have you ever thought about your don't-give-up story? It is a powerful reminder to others to trust God and persevere in faith. God wants your faith journey to encourage others in their faith walk.

Your story of God's faithfulness is exactly what someone else needs to hear today so they can see hope in the middle of their brokenness.

I purchased that beautiful art. It now hangs in the family room as a reminder that God takes our stories of hurt and pain and turns them into stories of redemption and hope.

Remember, this is not the end of your story, but just the beginning of God's story!

Do you believe God specializes in redemption?

Do you believe He can use your brokenness to point others back to Jesus?

Do you believe in the power of community?

In Tim Tebow's book, *Shaken*, he talks about the dash, the line that separates a person's birth from their death. After losing Jeannie, this dash seemed more important to me than ever. He wrote, "This tiny mark of punctuation represents what we stand for, what or whom we impact, and ultimately what legacy we leave behind."[58] Tim then encourages us to consider if we are living for ourselves or making a difference in the lives of others. "When we think about our dash, we can live with more passion. We can identify our priorities. We can be intentional in how we live. We can make a difference and do things that matter."[59]

Helping others in need, like we did for Jeannie's family, and allowing ourselves to be helped by others are ways to make our dash count. As I think about community and the large sequoia trees, I'm convinced that the interlocking of roots was God's plan all along. We are better linked together as we show Jesus's love in everything we do!

Let's Pray

> *God*, I want to be a bridge builder. I want to encourage those coming behind me and show gratitude to those in front of me who have offered their support and wisdom. Help me interlock roots with others and point people to Jesus. Give me compassion and empathy for those hurting and remind me that we are stronger together. In Jesus's name, Amen.

Truth

> Your story of God's faithfulness helps others find hope in the middle of their story of brokenness.

25

Hopelifter

Not only that, but we rejoice in our sufferings,
knowing that suffering produces endurance,
and endurance produces character,
and character produces hope,
and hope does not put us to shame,
because God's love has been poured
into our hearts through the Holy Spirit
who has been given to us.

Romans 5:3–5 ESV

I want to be a hopelifter!

Awaiting the arrival of my son from summer camp, I was surrounded by restless parents anxious for the bus to pull into the empty church parking lot. Standing on the sidewalk between the youth building and the hot black asphalt, we were all melting away under the scorching sun.

Trying to keep hydrated, I took a sip of water as my cell phone vibrated in my pocket. I gasped when I read the words on my phone. I was hoping to see an update from the junior high ministry staff with an ETA for our teenagers, but I was instead stunned by the heartbreaking message from my dear friend.

"My husband told me before he left this morning that he wants a divorce."

Her words pierced my soul. Suddenly, my annoyance about having to wait in the heat seemed utterly trivial. I read her text a second time, and all the hurt and pain I had felt after hearing similar words just two and a half years earlier flooded my mind.

I was shocked. Devastated. My heart shattered for my friend. Her world was turning upside down, and honestly, I could not think of a single adequate word to ease her pain. I decided the best choice was simply to let her know that she was not alone.

As we texted back and forth, she revealed that her husband was planning to move out that night, and they needed to tell the kids right away. Remembering how hard it was to share the same news with my kids, my spirit wept for my friend. I had been literally sick to my stomach the day we told my kids that their father was moving out.

Recalling all the tears and sadness, I assured her that I was praying for her and her children. Knowing the importance of the gift of being present, I drove to her house that night to deliver a care package to her. It featured a book, *When God Doesn't Fix It* by Laura Story, that had helped me during my divorce. I hoped it would offer her some hope in the middle of her heartache.

We stood out in front of her house that night and talked for about an hour. The reality that he had left and that she was now a single mom was hitting hard. Together, we cried over the loss for both her and her kids.

The next morning, I sent her another text. "I know yesterday was one of the hardest days of your life. I remember all the raw emotions I felt. My prayer for you today is that you will spend some time alone with God and just share all of it with Him. You can write in a journal or just speak to Him out loud. I found it so helpful. I would share my anger, my hurt, my sadness for my boys . . . all of it, and then I prayed and asked God for the strength to get through that day. I just did that over and over again, and God was faithful to walk through each day with me. Just know I will be praying for you constantly. Wish I can take all the pain away. I am here if you need to talk. Love you friend."

Oh, how I wish I could have taken away her hurt. Over the next couple of months, we talked several times a week. I listened as she shared her sorrowful emotions. I also told her parts of my story and validated how painful the rejection feels. Knowing I understood offered another layer of support. Like me, my friend was meeting with a counselor to help work through the pain, but it was helpful to process it with someone else who had walked a similar path.

As I vulnerably and genuinely told her about my experience and how God had helped me through my grief, it gave her hope.

Hope is a powerful thing. It can lift your spirits and allow you to see new possibilities. This is why I believe the psalmist repeated these hopeful words three times in consecutive chapters of the Psalms. "Why am I discouraged? Why is my heart so sad? I will put my hope in God! I will praise him again—my Savior and my God." The exact same words are reiterated in three different verses: Psalm 42:5, Psalm 42:11, and Psalm 43:5 (NLT).

Have you ever repeated something to your children or a loved one? Maybe it was because they were not listening. Perhaps it was because the words you were saying were so important that you did not want them to miss what you said. For me, I am constantly telling my boys that God made them for a purpose.

The truth in our words is so important that we will share it again so they will not forget.

I believe that is what is happening in Psalms 42 and 43. There is repetition because God does not want us to miss the importance of hope.

Brokenness can easily lead to hopelessness. The unexpected twists and turns of the world leave us feeling discouraged and disheartened. It could be that you are feeling this way right now, downcast from a doctor's diagnosis, reeling from a devastation in your marriage, or heartbroken from a choice your child is making.

Whatever it is, God knew that we would need to remember a vital truth as we walk through these tough seasons, so He had the psalmist repeat it multiple times.

Put your hope in God in the midst of the storm.

If you are struggling to find hope, I pray that God will bring you a hopelifter!

In Kathe Wunnenberg's book, *Hopelifter*, she defines hopelifters as "people who have been transformed by their own experience and grief and who are now willingly offering themselves as the hands and feet of Jesus to comfort other hurting hearts."[60]

We are all on a journey and have people ahead of us, next to us, and behind us. Sometimes we are the ones walking through the difficult circumstances, gleaning hope from someone else. Other times, God asks us to turn around and reach out our hand to a person behind us and say, *I have been there, and I want to help and encourage you as you walk through your unexpected storm.*

Has someone come alongside you and offered you hope? Do you have a hopelifter in your life? Did their story of how God met them in their pain encourage you in your faith?

Not only did she write the book, but my friend Kathe is a lovely example of a hopelifter. She "believes we go through what we go through to help others go through what we went through."[61] She models this beautifully every Mother's Day. Kathe has a heart for grieving moms because she has experienced the hurt of losing a baby. She does not waste her pain, but she lets God use her story of loss to help others and spread hope. One of my favorite ways she does this is her annual Hope on Wheels Mother's Day trip for grieving moms.

Kathe wrote, "We share a common bond and sisterhood of

loss. Some are fresh in their journey and preparing for their first Mother's Day without their child. Others are veteran sojourners, well familiar with suffering and this bus trip. Amazingly, God's power at work in and through their broken hearts spreads hope in the hearts of others."[62]

Please don't miss what she shared; it is God's power at work through these women. We cannot become a hopelifter in our strength. But as we rely on His power, He takes our broken pieces and uses them to touch the heart of someone else.

In her book, Kathe declares that the "hopelifters' presence, personal touch, prayers, practical advice, and individual stories of God's help and healing power in their own lives lifts other women and points them to the God of hope. And in time . . . those receiving hope will spread hope too."[63]

It is our presence that offers hope, our personal touch and prayers that touch hearts, and our practical advice and stories that give comfort. I love that we can be real with our pain, and God will use it in mighty ways.

Are you a hopelifter? Who do you need to reach out to? Who do you need to offer your presence and your story?

Don't wait! Today, I encourage you to write down the name of someone who is hurting and reach out to them this week. I promise you: you want to be hopelifter.

When I had the opportunity to interview Kathe on my podcast, she revealed something amazing. The women who first attend Hope on Wheels as a newly grieving mom usually return for the trip years later and offer hope to another mom who is just beginning her journey of loss. Because they had experienced firsthand receiving the help and hope of someone before them, they couldn't wait to come back and provide that same hope to someone behind them.

That is the power of hope! That is the beauty of a hopelifter!

Our healing comes full circle when we allow God to use our broken story to help another hurting heart.

Our healing comes full circle when we allow God to use our broken story to help another hurting heart.

Do you see your story as a gift to share with others? I love what Lysa TerKeurst shares in her book *It's Not Supposed To Be This Way*. She says, "There's someone else in the world who would drown in their own tears if not for seeing yours."[64]

You are the answer to someone else's prayer! Your willingness to vulnerably share your broken story will unleash hope into their broken story.

Are you ready for your mess to become your message? Do you want God to bring beauty to your ashes?

Friend, I still don't fully understand the *why* behind our grief. Walking through a divorce was not the plan I had for my life. But what I do know is that my story of divorce helped another mom walking through her divorce. My tears became my testimony. He wants to do the same for you.

Your personal example of how God was faithful and met you in your pain is exactly what another hurting heart needs to hear today. I want to encourage you to take a step of faith and share your story. Be a hopelifter!

Let's Pray

God, if I am honest, it is hard to tell others about my hurt and pain. But I believe it is my vulnerability about my struggles that allows me to deeply connect to another hurting heart. Help me be brave and share my broken story with someone behind me. God, use me to encourage and empower a grieving soul and offer them hope. In Jesus's name, Amen.

Truth

God takes your deepest pain and turns it into your greatest ministry.

26

Your God Story Is Powerful

They triumphed over him
by the blood of the Lamb and
by the word of their testimony.

Revelation 12:11

I am still in awe about how God used my story.

Across the globe in Rwanda, Africa, our Saddleback Church KSG team gathered in the large downstairs room at our hotel for our final morning meeting. My eyes scanned the faces of the re-markable boys and girls in the circle as we sang our favorite song, "Reckless Love."

Just eleven days earlier, Conor had graduated from elementary school. The following day, he and I boarded a plane with seven sixth grade child-and-parent duos. People that had started as mere acquaintances had since become lifelong friends after two long ten-hour plane rides and a full week of ministry.

Serving others in need in the country of Rwanda, previously known for its genocide but now recognized for its reconciliation and forgiveness, had undeniably bonded and changed us for the better.

As we visited preschools and churches as well as homes, our

incredible team enthusiastically shared the love of Jesus. Each day, we huddled to talk about how we saw God moving in people's lives. We enjoyed hearing students and adults tell their highs and lows. Our time in Rwanda had been exciting and fruitful, but as we began our final day there, we also realized it had been exhausting.

When we were done worshipping, our team leader, Liza, shared that we would be visiting Mama Joy's ministry as our last stop on the way to our debrief. Mama Joy helped women get off the streets by teaching them life skills like sewing and hairstyling. "I need one of you to teach a devotional or speak some words of encouragement to these women today," Liza offered. Knowing we were all emotionally and physically depleted from the long days of outreach, she added, "Please pray and ask God if He is calling you to share."

Honestly, as I walked back to my room, I was completely unaware of the God assignment right in front of me.

I plopped down on my bed and stretched out my tired muscles. Each day, we had labored for twelve hours. As I dragged myself to start packing for the journey home, my eyes caught a glimpse of my cracked clay pot.

I had brought that same pot with me to Rwanda four years before when I came with my older son, Kyle. Earlier that year, God had opened my eyes to the beauty in brokenness when I purposely cracked a ceramic piece in my backyard. Even though I was willing to tell my story, no opportunity had presented itself that trip, so the pot had come back home with me.

Now, as I stared at the pot again, I knew I had become a completely different woman. God had been growing me and developing within me a powerful message of hope born out of my difficulties. In my heart, I heard the Lord say, "Just like your clay pot, these women are broken. I want you to share your testimony on brokenness."

God was calling *me* to speak.

Honestly, part of me wanted to run away in fear. For a split second, I thought, *No one else knows that God asked me to tell my story.* But I knew that I would regret it if I refused to be faithful in His direction, regardless of how tired or scared I might be.

Picking up my broken pot, I went and found my team leader. "Has anyone else felt called to share to the women?" She shook her head. I showed her my pot and explained what I felt God wanted me to say.

"You are on when we get there," she happily confirmed.

To say that I was nervous was an understatement. I had never before stood in front of a group of women and shared my story. Emotions heightened, my eyes kept filling with tears as I boarded the bus to head to Mama Joy's.

At first, I thought I was feeling concerned about whether or not I was prepared, but as I sat quietly and reflected, I knew deep in my heart that God had been preparing me for a long time. Thinking through what I'd written in my recent blog posts on brokenness, I realized God was just asking me to share the life message that I'd already been writing about.

God never wastes a hurt! He specializes in turning our pain into His purpose.

All I had to do was trust that He would give me the specific words to speak to the precious African women.

So, in a tiny alley on the streets of Rwanda, I poured out my heart and shared my broken story. Holding up my cracked clay pot, I told them how my world had been turned upside down and inside out when I had my miscarriage and how my heart had been shattered into a million pieces when I went through my divorce. Through it all, I declared how God's love and comfort had met me in the middle of my heartbreak.

With fresh tears, I encouraged the women to remember that God would take their brokenness and turn it into something beautiful. The horrible circumstances they had endured, the painful moments they had felt alone, the tears they had shed—God would not waste any of it.

There was not a dry eye as I shared about God's faithfulness in the midst of our storms.

The broken pot that had traveled to Rwanda with me two different times was a powerful visual for these women of the beauty to be found in their brokenness. "God's light shines brightest through our cracks and broken places," I said. That message of hope sank deeply into their hearts.

What if God could use their broken story?

What if God could bring purpose to their pain?

What if their brokenness could help them be a stronger light for Jesus?

Friend, I want you to reflect on those same questions. What if God can use *your* broken story? What if God wants to bring purpose to *your* pain? What if *your* brokenness helps you be a stronger light for Jesus?

After I finished my testimony, I walked over and hugged the women. I also left the broken clay pot behind with them as a reminder that God could use their broken story.

The Bible says,

> We now have this light shining in our hearts, but we ourselves are like fragile clay jars containing this great treasure. This makes it clear that our great power is from God, not from ourselves. We are pressed on every side by troubles, but we are not crushed. We are perplexed, but not driven to despair. We are hunted down, but never abandoned by God. We get knocked down, but we are not destroyed. (2 Corinthians 4:7–9 NLT).

If you are feeling knocked down, perplexed, and pressed on every side, here is some encouragement that Pastor Buddy Owens pointed out in a sermon at Saddleback Church. "Do you notice in these verses that there are commas after each descriptive word, not a period?"

The NIV version reads,

- We are hard pressed on every side [comma], but not crushed.
- Perplexed [comma], but not in despair.
- Persecuted [comma], but not abandoned.
- Struck down [comma], but not destroyed.

"Never put a period where God places a comma."[65]

My heart leaped with encouragement as I heard those hope-filled words from my pastor. If you are struggling to see any light amid the dark, maybe you need to hear them too.

A period signifies the end of a sentence, but a comma shows that there is still more to come. What would happen if we chose to view our brokenness that way? Right now, you may be feeling only grief and confusion. You are hard pressed and perplexed, but those emotions are not the end of your story. With God's strength, you can exchange the period you placed at the end of your difficult circumstance with a comma.

What is a practical way to do this? First, write out how you are feeling. Then cross out the period and exchange it for a comma. Then add a paraphrase of one of the "I know" verses in the Bible or a favorite Scripture verse. I then highly recommend you speak those statements out loud with passion!

I cannot see how God can bring anything good from this (comma), but I know that God causes everything to work together for the good of those who love God and are called according to his purpose for them (Romans 8:28).

I feel lost with no plan (comma), but I know God has plans to prosper me not to harm me, and He plans to give me hope and a future (Jeremiah 29:11).

I am struggling to trust God through these uncertain times

(comma), but I can trust the Lord with all my heart and lean not on my own understanding. In all my ways, I can acknowledge Him, and He will direct my paths (Proverbs 3:5–6).

When I shared my personal story that special day in Rwanda, I was really sharing God's story of redemption in my life.

God wants to redeem your story too. He has a plan bigger than you can even imagine, and He wants you to trust Him even when you cannot understand. Fall back into His loving arms today, and ask Him to give you His strength as you walk through your difficult season.

The word *through* is key. Think back to the STRENGTH acrostic in this book. As you Seek Him and invite Him into your pain, He will help you Tearfully grieve and heal from your emotions. He will then help you Replace your finite view with His infinite perspective. Through it all, He wants you to Embrace His character development, and Never lose sight of His amazing grace. I hope that you can Give God praise even in the middle of the storm, and Trust God is good even when you don't understand. Most of all, I pray you will Honestly share your broken story and help another hurting heart.

This is not the end of your story, but the beginning of an even greater story. Your God story is powerful!

As I look back on my God story, I can see how each heartbreak has taught me a valuable life-changing lesson. God used the miscarriage to reveal my life verse, 2 Corinthians 1:3–4, which reminds me that God comforts us so we can then go and comfort others. The important message that God never wastes our hurts was birthed that summer, along with my book ministry.

The divorce taught me so many lessons on brokenness. Like the cracked clay pot, God's light can shine brightest through our broken places as we lay them at His feet and He turns them into something beautiful. He also showed me that others will connect more with our struggles than with our successes, and He encouraged me to be more vulnerable and share my testimony.

Last, God grew my roots deeper in Him with each heartbreak. The title *Depth* came to me the summer before my best friend passed away from cancer. Her loss revealed to me that heartbreak can catapult me to growth and depth in my faith.

Even though I would not have chosen any of them, each difficulty made me into the woman I am today. They birthed a ministry. A blog. A podcast. A book. Speaking opportunities. All to help you in the middle of your storm, to offer you hope and encourage you to grow deeper in your faith and stronger in your relationships.

None of these would exist if I had not walked through my greatest heartbreaks.

What is God desiring to birth inside you as you give Him the broken pieces of your life? How is God catapulting you to deeper growth in Him?

I don't believe we can journey from heartbreak to strength and then stay the same on the inside. I believe God is placing a calling on your life. He wants to use you. Not just the gifts He has given you, but the pain and suffering too.

> **I don't believe we can journey from heartbreak to strength and then stay the same on the inside.**

In his book *Soul Keeping*, John Ortberg wrote, "If you ask people who don't believe in God why they don't, the number one reason will be suffering. If you ask people who believe in God when they grew most spiritually, the number one answer will be suffering."[66]

My desire is that as you close the last page of this book, you will find yourself in that latter group with a glimmer of hope in your eyes as you see how God can take your greatest heartbreak and catapult you to your greatest growth!

This is not the easier path. It involves full surrender to your Creator and faith and trust beyond what sometimes makes sense. But this avenue leads to greater depth and strength in God.

This route also shines bright with God's redemption and nearness. As He turns pain into purpose, His loving arms wrap around you with comfort and peace beyond understanding. Knowing He is working behind the scenes and His perspective is infinitely clearer than what your limited sight can see, you can begin to replace the period at the end of the sentence with a comma.

Each layer of trust leads to added layers of depth with Him as you expectantly wait for what the Lord has in store for you.

God wants to take you from a place of heartbreak to strength! He desires to grow your roots deeper than ever before. I hope that you will let Him!

Let's Pray

> *God*, help me fully trust You with my heartbreak. I don't want to stay the same—I want to grow deeper in my relationship with You. Help me remember You are not finished with my story. Give me Your daily strength when the fog of grief comes rolling in. Place people in my life to support and encourage me along this growth path. Finally, God, thank You for your redemptive plan to give beauty for my ashes and purpose for my pain. In Jesus's name, Amen.

Truth

> This is not the end of your story, but the beginning of an even greater story.

Acknowledgments

God-sized dreams cannot be accomplished on our own. We need strength and wisdom from our heavenly Father as well as love and support from family and friends to make it happen. I would love to recognize those who comforted me in the middle of the tears, answered my early morning calls to listen to what God was revealing, and encouraged me in both the valleys and the peaks of this publishing journey.

God, I never could have made this dream a reality without You guiding me. This whole process has taught me the importance of depending on You for all my needs and inspiration. The words *in awe of God* frequently left my lips as I saw Your hand directing me and presiding over the words chosen in this book.

Kyle and Conor, you are the most amazing sons. I can think back to the years in counseling, and I was just barely a step ahead of you in learning how to name and manage my emotions. Thank you for your patience with me and for together embracing, "My response is my responsibility." I believe the loss you experienced has grown and shaped you into remarkable men with a deep compassion and empathy toward others. I am so proud of both of you.

Mom and Dad, thank you for your support over the years.

From cheering me on in my writing, to being guests on my podcast, to listening to my highs and lows. I am grateful for your love and encouragement!

To my three wonderful sisters. Jill, thank you for your listening ears and loving care when my world was shattering. Julie, I have cherished our deep conversations about emotional literacy and our mutual desire to grow from our heartbreaks. Jamie, thank you for always celebrating each exciting step with a "Woohoo" text and for your inspiring words like, "Someday someone is going to be just as excited to meet you and get their book signed by you."

To my friends who supported me during the hardest year of my life. I don't know how many times you took my phone calls as I circled the park with tears flowing down my cheeks. You listened with empathy, prayed for God's comfort and wisdom, and our conversations gave me hope to keep leaning into God. I am forever grateful for Erin, Yvonne, Meredith, Anita, Kerri, and Wendy, and how you met me in my pain and lifted me up. Thank you for continuing to cheer me on as God gave me the book idea!

It truly takes a village to birth a book. In addition to the names above, I want to give a special thanks to Karyce, Moana, Michelle, Christy, Kerry, and Joy, for listening to my ups and downs on the road to publishing. To Noelle, Maile, Kathy, Heather, and Kim, for offering feedback on the words in these pages. To Lois, Lisa, Lesley, Nikki, Krista, and Debbie, for your words of encouragement along the way. To Susan, Laurie, Allison, Elizabeth, and my small group, for your prayers over this book. Every one of you celebrated each exciting milestone with me. I am forever grateful for these priceless gifts. For those who are not mentioned, but are in my heart, you know who you are.

To Sophia and Lucas, thank you for letting me share about your precious mom, Jeannie. She was an incredible friend who not only helped me through my miscarriage, but also was a huge support during my divorce. I miss you so much, Jeannie. Please give

Baby Grace a hug and kiss from me, and I will do the same for you here with your kids. Also, to Marisa, thank you for sitting with me on the couch as I cried over the loss of my baby.

Kathe Wunnenberg, thank you for being an amazing mentor and speaking truth into my life. Your books, *Grieving the Child I Never Knew* and *Hopelifter,* were not only pivotal in my growth, but God used them to connect us on my podcast. Your wisdom and support have been an integral part of this book coming to fruition. Thank you for your beautiful words in the foreword and for your Spirit-led commission during the Time to Dream Retreat.

To my wonderful counselor Debbie. Thank you for the years of wisdom and insight as I sat in front of you on your couch and poured out my hurting heart. I am grateful for the connections you helped me make from my past to present. My emotional literacy grew exponentially as we identified my triggers and made growth steps. Thank you for being a huge part in my healing.

Adam Colwell at WriteWorks, you are a phenomenal book coach! Not only did you help me see redundancies in my writing, but you guided and taught me how to "show not tell" in my story writing. I am forever grateful for your brilliant edits on this book and your patience and persistence to move my writing to a new level.

To my hope*writers friends. Thank you, Becky, for your encouraging phone calls, and Lisa, for believing in me and asking me to share part of my story in your book as well as be part of your Hope in Grief Team. To my IG group. I cannot begin to express my gratitude for all of you and your extraordinary support!

Danya, thank you for encouraging me to attend She Speaks and write weekly on my blog in 2018. This choice drastically changed the course of my writing as God improved my skills through this consistent act of surrender each week. Praying for God's words each Tuesday night and seeing His faithfulness every Wednesday morning truly was a catalyst to pray bolder prayers for the words in this book.

A special thank you to Lysa TerKeurst and the P31 Bootcamp. I am grateful for your remarkable teaching videos and expertise in all things writing and publishing as well as your Compel training on how to write a sticky statement. Also, I appreciate Nicki Koziarz, my bootcamp coach, for your honest feedback on the outline of my book and Melissa, Sonia, and Jennifer, for your magnificent editing on my value statements, author's promise, and book hooks.

To Cindy Lambert, thank you for your wise counsel to change the title of my book. In six words, you captured the entire book, and I am extremely grateful for your insight. In addition, thank you Cherie for your inspiring idea for my logo, Cat for implementing it, and Jeff for redesigning my website.

I am also grateful to all my podcast guests for sharing how God took their greatest heartbreak and catapulted them to their greatest growth. In addition, I am appreciative for my Heartbreak to Strength guest writers on my blog. Thanks to all of you for your powerful stories of hope and God's faithfulness.

To the Redemption Press Team. Thank you for believing in my book and helping guide me through the entire publication process.

So many people played an important role in this book, so from the bottom of my heart, thank you for your love, support, and encouragement!

Love, Jodi

Appendix A

Ten Verses to Help Encourage Your Hurting Heart

God wants you to know He is leaning in close to you and your broken heart.

> "The Lord is close to the brokenhearted and saves those who are crushed in spirit." (Psalm 34:18)

God wants you to know that you are not facing this alone.

> "Be strong and courageous. Do not be afraid or terrified because of them, for the Lord your God goes with you; he will never leave you nor forsake you." (Deuteronomy 31:6)

God wants you to give His peace in exchange for your troubled heart.

> "My peace I give you . . . Do not let your hearts be troubled." (John 14:27)

God wants you not to worry; He is bigger than your problem.

> "The Lord is near. Do not be anxious about anything." (Philippians 4:5–6)

God wants to provide and meet your needs.

> "My God will meet all your needs according to the riches of his glory in Christ Jesus." (Philippians 4:19)

God wants to walk alongside you through your storm.

> "Fear not, for I have redeemed you; I have called you by name, you are mine. When you pass through the waters, I will be with you; and through the rivers, they shall not overwhelm you; when you walk through fire you shall not be burned, and the flame shall not consume you. For I am the Lord your God, the Holy One of Israel, your Savior." (Isaiah 43:1–3 ESV)

God wants to strengthen you and help you in your times of trouble.

> "God is our refuge and strength, an ever-present help in trouble. Therefore, we will not fear, though the earth give way and the mountains fall into the heart of the sea, though its waters roar and foam and the mountains quake with their surging." (Psalm 46:1–3)

God wants you to know He hears you as you cry out to Him.

> "But I will call on God, and the LORD will rescue me. Morning, noon, and night I cry out in my distress, and the LORD hears my voice." (Psalm 55:16-17 NLT)

God wants you to place your hope in Him and seek Him each morning.

> "Because of the LORD's great love we are not consumed, for his compassions never fail. They are new every morning; great is your faithfulness. I say to myself, "The LORD is my portion; therefore I will wait for him." The LORD is good to those whose hope is in him, to the one who seeks him; it is good to wait quietly for the salvation of the LORD." (Lamentations 3:22–26)

God wants to comfort you in your grief, so that you can comfort another hurting heart.

> "Praise be to the God and Father of our Lord Jesus Christ, the Father of compassion and the God of all comfort, who comforts us in all our troubles, so that we can comfort those in any trouble with the comfort we ourselves receive from God." (2 Corinthians 1:3–4)

Appendix B

Ten Steps to Help You Through the Holidays

Grieving the loss of a loved one is hard, but Holidays without your loved ones is the hardest.

Since Holidays have a way of magnifying our grief, let me encourage you by sharing some things that helped me during my grief.

1. **Give yourself lots of grace** if you are missing someone special this Thanksgiving.

2. **Ask God for strength and energy to get through the day.** Invite friends to pray for you too.

3. **Surround yourself with people who care and can empathize with you.** This could be your family, friends, or your small group at church.

4. **Be honest with how you are feeling and let others know what you need.** Journal how you are feeling if that helps!

5. **Talk about the loved one you are missing.** Let yourself cry if needed; I remember shedding lots of tears.

6. **Don't put any expectations on yourself** to do the same traditions you have done in the past if it is too much for you.

7. **Guard your heart by taking a social media break**. Social Media makes you think that everyone has it all together, and you are the only one whose life has been shattered.

8. **Fill your mind with truth** by listening to worship music or reading a helpful book.

9. **Please don't rush your grief**. Don't worry about anyone else's expectations. You set your pace for the day.

10. **And most importantly, remember that "It is okay not to be okay."**

I know how hard it is to miss a loved one this holiday, so I will be praying for you as God helps you get through this day. Sending you a big hug!

Love, Jodi

Endnotes

Chapter 3

1 Max Lucado, *Anxious for Nothing: Finding Calm in a Chaotic World* (Nashville: Thomas Nelson, 2017), 8.

2 Lucado, 121.

Chapter 4

3 Mark Batterson, *The Circle Maker: Praying Circles Around Your Biggest Dreams and Greatest Fears* (Grand Rapids: Zondervan, 2011, 2016), 19, 91.

4 Batterson, 65.

Chapter 5

5 Rick Warren, "How to Deal With How You Feel," February 15–16, 2014, https://saddleback.com/watch/50-days-of-transformation/how-to-deal-with-how-you-feel.

6 Philip Yancey, "Easter at Columbine," https://philipyancey.com/easter-at-columbine.

7 Philip Yancey, *The Question That Never Goes Away: Why* (Grand Rapids: Zondervan, 2013), 128.

Chapter 6

8 Jason Gray, "The Story behind 'Death Without a Funeral'," YouTube Video, 3:34, June 30, 2016, https://youtu.be/Jul16uQ85bg.

9 Brené Brown, "Brené Brown on Empathy and Sympathy," YouTube Video, 2:53, April 1, 2016, https://youtu.be/KZBTYViDPlQ.

10 Brown, "Brené Brown on Empathy and Sympathy."

11 Poem written by Holley Gerth © DaySpring Cards. Used by permission.

Chapter 7

12 Grief.com, "The 5 Stages of Grief," https://grief.com/the-five-stages-of-grief/.

13 Grief.com, "The 5 Stages of Grief."

14 Christina Gregory, "The Five Stages of Grief: An Examination of the

Kubler-Ross Model," Psycom, April 14, 2022, https://www.psycom.net/depression.central.grief.html.

15 Levi Lusko, *Through The Eyes of a Lion: Facing Impossible Pain, Finding Incredible Power* (Nashville: W Publishing Group, an imprint of Thomas Nelson, 2015), 82.

16 Lusko, *Through The Eyes of a Lion: Facing Impossible Pain, Finding Incredible Power*, 82.

Chapter 9

17 Suzie Eller, *The Mended Heart: God's Healing for Your Broken Places* (Ada, Mich: Revell, 2014), 55–56.

18 Lysa TerKeurst, *It's Not Supposed To Be This Way: Finding Unexpected Strength when Disappointments Leave You Shattered* (Nashville: Thomas Nelson, 2018), 16–17.

19 TerKeurst, 17.

20 TerKeurst, 18.

21 Holley Gerth, *Under God's Umbrella: Gifts of Hope and Encouragement to Shelter Your Heart in Life's Storms (Inspired Gifts)* (Nashville: Ellie Claire, an imprint of Worthy Publishing Group, 2013), 32–33.

Chapter 10

22 Karen Ehman, *Let It Go: How to Stop Running the Show and Start Walking in Faith* (Grand Rapids: Zondervan, 2012), 192.

Chapter 11

23 Mark Hall, *Thrive: Digging Deep, Reaching Out* (Grand Rapids: Zondervan, 2014), 15.

24 Tony Evans, *Detours: The Unpredictable Path to Your Destiny* (Nashville: B&H Publishing Group, 2017), 100–101.

25 Evans, 101–102.

Chapter 12

26 Milan & Kay Yerkovich, *How We Love Our Kids: The 5 Love Styles of Parenting* (Colorado Springs: Waterbrook, 2011), Chapter 5.

27 Lysa TerKeurst, *Unglued: Making Wise Choices in the Midst of Raw Emotions,* (Nashville, Nelson Books, 2014)

28 Lysa TerKeurst, *Forgiving What You Can't Forget: Discover How to*

Move On, Make Peace with Painful Memories, and Create a Life that's Beautiful Again (Nashville: Nelson Books, 2020), 72.

29 TerKeurst, 69.

30 TerKeurst, 84.

Chapter 13
31 C. S. Lewis, *The Problem of Pain* (New York: Harper Collins, 1940, 1996), 91.

Chapter 14
32 Lisa Bevere, *Girls With Swords: How to Carry Your Cross Like A Hero* (Colorado Springs: Waterbrook Press, 2013), 6–7.

33 *The Terminator*, James Cameron, Orion Pictures, 1984.

Chapter 15
34 Brené Brown, *Daring Greatly: How the Courage to Be Vulnerable Transforms the Way We Live, Love, Parent, and Lead* (New York: Avery, 2012), 33–34.

Chapter 16
35 Sheila Walsh, *The Storm Inside: Trade the Chaos of How You Fell for the Truth of Who You Are* (Nashville: Nelson Books, 2017), 51.

36 Lysa TerKeurst, *Forgiving What You Can't Forget: Discover How to Move On, Make Peace with Painful Memories, and Create a Life that's Beautiful Again* (Nashville: Nelson Books, 2020), 45.

37 TerKeurst, 26.

Chapter 17
38 Rick Warren, "Trusting God Through Gratitude," https://pastorrick.com/.

39 Warren, "Trusting God Through Gratitude."

40 Melissa Spoelstra, *The Names of God: His Character Revealed* (Nashville: Abingdon Women 2020), 204.

Chapter 18
41 Casting Crowns, "Praise You In This Storm." Beach Street and Reunion Records, 2005.

42 Ann Voskamp, *One Thousand Gifts: A Dare to Live Fully Right Where You Are* (Grand Rapids: Zondervan, 2010), 33.

Chapter 20

43 Craig Groeschel, *Hope in the Dark: Believing God Is Good When Life Is Not* (Grand Rapids: Zondervan, 2018), 21.

44 Socrates Perez, "Your Will Be Done," Saddleback Worship, 2016.

45 Craig Groeschel, *Hope in the Dark: Believing God Is Good When Life Is Not* (Grand Rapids: Zondervan, 2018), 113.

Chapter 21

46 Tony Evans, *Detours: The Unpredictable Path to Your Destiny.* (Nashville: B&H Publishing Group, 2017), 19, 21.

47 Evans, 52.

48 Evans, 22.

49 Randy Frazee, *The Heart of the Story: God's Masterful Design to Restore His People* (Grand Rapids: Zondervan, 2011, 2017), 60.

Chapter 22

50 Lysa TerKeurst, "First Samuel," First 5 app, Proverbs 31 Ministries, www.First5.org.

Chapter 24

51 Vivian Mabuni, *Open Hands Willing Heart: Discover the Joy of Saying Yes to God* (Colorado Springs: Waterbrook, 2019), 136.

52 Lysa TerKeurst, *Who Holds the Key to Your Heart?* (Chicago: Moody Publishers, 2002), 98.

53 TerKeurst, 101.

54 Christine Caine, https://twitter.com/christinecaine/status/1263986047379058688.

55 Kyle Idleman, *Don't Give Up: Faith that Gives You the Confidence to Keep Believing and the Courage to Keep Going* (Ada, Michigan: Baker Books, 2019), 24.

56 Idleman, 30.

57 Idleman, 31.

58 Tim Tebow, *Shaken: Discovering Your True Identity in the Midst of Life's Storms* (Colorado Springs: Waterbrook, 2016), 193.

59 Tebow, 193.

Chapter 25

60 Kathe Wunnenberg, *Hopelifter: Creative Ways to Spread Hope When Life Hurts* (Grand Rapids: Zondervan, 2013), 19.

61 Wunnenberg, 20.

62 Wunnenberg, 19.

63 Wunnenberg, 19.

64 Lysa TerKeurst, *It's Not Supposed To Be This Way: Finding Unexpected Strength when Disappointments Leave You Shattered* (Nashville: Thomas Nelson, 2018), 221.

Chapter 26

65 Buddy Owens, *Trusting God Through Trouble*, November 10–11, 2018, https://saddleback.com/watch/trusting-god-through-trouble/trusting-god-through-trouble.

66 John Ortberg, *Soul Keeping: Caring for the Most Important Part of You* (Grand Rapids: Zondervan, 2014), 179.

ORDER INFORMATION

REDEMPTION
PRESS

To order additional copies of this book, please visit
www.redemption-press.com.
Also available at Christian bookstores and Barnes and Noble.

CPSIA information can be obtained
at www.ICGtesting.com
Printed in the USA
JSHW060134170822
29382JS00004B/17